The SAND Room

Searching And Noticing the Divine

Volume 1

DIANE C. SHORE

Shore
Anything is possible when
you follow the Son!
Publishing

Copyright © 2015 Diane C. Shore

All rights reserved.

ISBN: 0990523136
ISBN-13: 978-0-9905231-3-0

Scripture quotations marked (NIV) are taken from the Holy Bible, New International Version®, NIV®. Copyright © 1973, 1978, 1984, 2011 by Biblica, Inc.™ Used by permission of Zondervan. All rights reserved worldwide. www.zondervan.com The "NIV" and "New International Version" are trademarks registered in the United States Patent and Trademark Office by Biblica, Inc.™

Scripture taken from the New King James Version®. Copyright © 1982 by Thomas Nelson. Used by permission. All rights reserved.

Scripture quotations are taken from the Holy Bible, New Living Translation, copyright ©1996, 2004, 2007, 2013 by Tyndale House Foundation. Used by permission of Tyndale House Publishers, Inc., Carol Stream, Illinois 60188. All rights reserved.

DEDICATION

Dedicated to the Holy Spirit, for opening my
eyes each day to the wondrous workings of God.

CONTENTS

	Acknowledgments	1
	Introduction	3
1	The Boy and the Snake	6
2	Even Jesus	8
3	A Heavenly Treasure Hunt	10
4	The Lake	12
5	The Simple Things	14
6	It's All Good	16
7	Looking Back	18
8	What Have We Missed?	20
9	Intermingled	22
10	Why Wait?	24
11	An Open Wound	26
12	Searching the Scriptures	28
13	I'm Going Home!	30
14	Blessings	32
15	Ready! Set! Go!	34
16	A GRAND-Parent's Love	36
17	She said, "No!"	38

18	Divine Moments	40
19	Anything?	42
20	Being Guarded!	44
21	A Trip Home	46
22	What Does God Sound Like?	48
23	One of the Devil's Lies	50
24	I Saw Jesus Today!	52
25	Does God Care About Football?	54
26	Offer Up a Prayer!	56
27	Pray or be Prey!	58
28	Thank You, Lord!	60
29	Dedicated to You, Jesus	62
30	Oh, Holy Night	64
31	Surprise!	70
32	The Open Door	72
33	We Prayed A Lot	74
34	Undeserved	76
35	What Do You See?	78
36	My Bad!	80
37	Pray and Wait	82
38	Where's Your Bible?	84

How the stories from The SAND Room began…

39	Gifts of Love	86
40	One Pair of Shoes	88
41	Whose Scent Are We Wearing?	90
42	Let's Take a Walk!	92
43	Is Your Gas Light On?	94
44	Such a Little Thing	96
45	A New Perspective	98
46	The Very Reason	102
47	The Year Was…	104
48	Prove To Me That You Love Me	106
49	What Are Your Needs?	108
50	The Luggage Rack Man	110
51	The Blessings of Obedience	112
52	Sea Turtles	114
	About the Author	116

ACKNOWLEDGMENTS

Thank You to the Father,
because You loved us enough to send us Your Son.

Thank You to Jesus,
because You loved us enough to
come into this world and save us.

Thank You to the Holy Spirit,
for living inside of us, and giving us the strength to carry on.

To all of you who let me share your stories in this book, I thank you.

Connie Dixon, your editing skills bless me!
I appreciate all the time and effort you put into these stories.

To my husband, Jim, thank you! Because of your efforts in
publishing these stories, they have a chance to be shared.

INTRODUCTION

How the stories from The SAND Room began...

We all want to see God, don't we? It would make it so much easier to believe that God really exists if we could actually see Him...and yet, when He *does* show up in our day-to-day experiences, do we notice Him? Do we acknowledge Him? Do we thank Him? Or do we just chalk these extraordinary events up to luck? Coincidence? Or our stars aligning just right on that day? In this book of short stories, we will **S**earch **A**nd **N**otice the **D**ivine together.

Perhaps you have been a part of a *long* journey with me and my writings, one that started in the darkest days any parent could have, the death of a precious child. If you've read along with me through the years, hopefully you saw a transformation of my heart. God took my shattered heart, and He carefully and painstakingly put it back together again. It wasn't an easy job—only a Mighty God could accomplish such a feat!

Through the years, I wrote, and I wrote, and I wrote, until I thought maybe my "writer" had worn out, and so I stopped. I thought maybe it was time. Eleven years, and possibly a million or more words later, was there anything left to say? We had moved out of our RV after ten years and put down roots. God provided a place for family gatherings now that we have six grandchildren. We are both working, and I have started drawing again, a pastime that used to fill many enjoyable hours in my days. And yet, writing still lingered there in the background of my mind...maybe I should just be making notes to pass on to my grandchildren if nothing else? I see God everywhere, every day. Shouldn't it be noted somewhere? I thought of how Moses kept reminding God's people in

Deuteronomy to not forget all that God had done for them as they wandered through the wilderness for the past 40 years. We don't want to forget those things!

While still pondering all this for several months, a wonderful lady visited our town. She is the aunt of one of my very special friends. Let's call her, Connie, since that is her name. Connie is a woman I had never met, but someone who has read a great deal of my writings. She urged me to continue writing. I was still wavering. She strongly urged me to continue writing, but I still wasn't fully convinced. I still thought maybe that season had passed. She even more strongly urged me to write!...and then came the day of, "The Boy and the Snake." It seemed Connie's prompting had turned into God's prompting in the very same week—and so begins a new chapter of life, with a new chapter of writings.

Connie helped me see that maybe a new format might be called for. Again, I pondered that. What is it God might be asking me to do here? I wasn't really sure, but it seemed today that I needed to "take a few steps into the river" before God was going to do something with what was flowing, as is written about in Joshua 3:8. Then, and only then, would He show the way. So, I picked up my laptop and began, and this is my very first *foot* in the river of writing again that you see in front of you. I'm taking that first step of faith and waiting with you to see what God has planned. I don't really know...

God is very active in our lives, if we will be available to see Him. I just picked up a book I have sitting here. In the book, it's talking about all the things in a day we can give thanks for. It reminds me to take notice And there it is! God just met me in the river of writing! God let me know we have to be *looking* for Him to *see* Him in our every day, otherwise we can miss the very subtle ways that He loves on us.

Since these writings now come to you from the room in our home I call the Sand Room, because of its color and the décor, I thought maybe it would be part of the title of this new season of writings. I didn't know how, or what SAND would mean, and God just gave that to me--we have to be: ***Searching And Noticing the Divine***. God is already meeting me here in the river! "But as soon as the feet of the priests who were carrying the Ark touched the water at the river's edge, the water began piling up..." Joshua 3:15,16. Thank you Lord Almighty. You are awesome!

On this day, as Paul Harvey would say, I will leave you with the "rest of the story" about *The Boy and the Snake*, since it is my jumping off point in sharing how God shows up in our every day, as He's just shown up in mine God is so good and so fun! I *will* continue to write and share how God shows up every day in so many amazing ways! Let's cross on over to the other side, and begin...

1

The Boy and the Snake

Snakes…not my favorite subject. So why do I start off this new series of writings with such a story? Because, I hope these new writings will be filled with stories of blessings beyond measure…stories of seeing God in our everyday circumstances and marveling at who He is and all the ways He shows Himself to us.

Today's story is a simple one, yet so like our God. We were visiting the San Francisco Zoo this last Sunday to celebrate our grandson, Jackson's, seventh birthday. We were there to see Jackson's present fascination, the Anaconda. For the past six months, that has been all Jackson wanted for his birthday—to take his best buddy, also named Jackson, to see the Anaconda that is at the San Francisco Zoo. His mother explained on the way to the zoo that he needed to be patient. We were going to see lots of other animals on the way to where the Anaconda was, but we would get there!

The big moment arrived, and we entered the building to see this very large snake. It was curled up in the water over in the corner of the window, and Jackson was thrilled! There it was at long last! Our very scientific grandson was elated! And we took many pictures, but the snake did nothing but lay still, as snakes do for the most part. Then Jackson asked his mom if he could take some pictures of the snake. He moved to the other window that was farther away from the snake, mostly because there were many people who wanted to get up close and see this snake. And then it happened! The snake started to make its way over to Jackson, to where he was behind the glass. It swam right up to him and seemed to be looking right at him! After six months of waiting, which is a long time for a small child, he saw his Anaconda just inches away!

God knew the desires of Jackson's heart, and He fulfilled his birthday wish in a most spectacular way! Jackson's day was fully complete as his long awaited desire was not only met, but even exceeded by our mighty God. Who else can move a snake but the One who created it?

Because of **S**earching **A**nd **N**oticing the **D**ivine, we saw what only God could do!

> *Take delight in the Lord, and he will*
> *give you your heart's desires.*
> Psalm 37:4 (NIV)

2

Even Jesus

Even in the life of Jesus, we see God showing up. Now that may seem like a strange sentence, and a strange thought, since Jesus is God. Why wouldn't we "see" God in Jesus' life? But the other day while reading Luke 4, I saw God show up in the happenings in the synagogue.

Here's what it says in Luke: *When he (Jesus) came to the village of Nazareth, his boyhood home, he went as usual to the synagogue on the Sabbath and stood up to read the Scriptures. The scroll, containing the messages of Isaiah the prophet, was handed to him, and he unrolled the scroll to the place where it says*:

> *"The Spirit of the Lord is upon me, for he has appointed me to preach Good News to the poor. He has sent me to proclaim that captives will be released, that the blind will see, that the downtrodden will be freed from their oppressors, and that the time of the Lord's favor has come."*

Did you see God there? Did you see what was *handed* to Jesus? The messages of Isaiah. Now granted, there were fewer messages at that time that had been written down, and I don't know what each scroll contained. Was it one small part or the whole of Isaiah? But whether it was or wasn't, Jesus was *handed* the scroll that described Him perfectly. On that day, Father God, from Heaven above, provided Son God, on Earth below, with the perfect reading for His introduction to His ministry.

It goes on to say:

> *He rolled up the scroll, handed it back to the attendant, and sat down. Everyone in the synagogue stared at him intently. Then He said, "This Scripture has come true today before your very eyes!"*

No big fanfare on Jesus' part, just simply said. And if you read this story further, you will see that those gathered there not only didn't believe what Jesus was saying, but Jesus went on to tell them some things that made them furious enough to mob Jesus and take Him to the edge of a hill and try to push Him over the cliff. Obviously, He escaped!

Things work as God designs them. Jesus introduced Himself to those in attendance in the synagogue, and He did so with confidence in who He was, is, and is to come! Jesus had become well known around Galilee.

> *He taught in their synagogues and was praised by everyone.*
> Luke 4:15

But when He took it a step further, or should we say when Father God took Him a step further and guided the Words of Isaiah into His hands that day, that was **bold**. It was also astonishing to those who knew Him only as Joseph's son. God was showing up big time! Most people missed it. And most didn't like it! Jesus went on His way to perform miracles in other places where He would be accepted and believed.

How often are we part of "the most" who miss what God so lovingly *hands* us?

When **S**earching **A**nd **N**oticing the **D**ivine, look for hidden nuggets everywhere!

3

A Heavenly Treasure Hunt

Ever gone looking for something and you can't find it? How about your keys…or your cell phone? Or even bigger than that…ever gone looking for your life in Jesus, and you can't seem to find it?

Today I went on a search for the Heavenly Treasure of being in a relationship with Jesus. How does one start? Is Jesus in the beauty of the songbirds on our patio? Is He in our morning coffee, and contentment it brings? Of course, He's in each of these examples, but is He somewhere deeper than that? How do we go about **S**earching **A**nd **N**oticing the **D**ivine when God seems elusive? Do we hunt for Jesus like He needs to be discovered? Sometimes I believe God wants us to **search** for Him like that because He knows when we do, we WILL find how gloriously wonderful He is and how very close He always is!

This morning, before I even knew I was on a heavenly treasure hunt, I saw glimpses of Jesus in the Word. I was being told about His place of rest. Then again, I saw Him come in close when the prayers for a friend of mine had been answered. Even more markers pointed towards Him in a book about transformed lives that I was reading. C.G Trumbull wrote, "Jesus Christ does not want to be our helper; He wants to be our life…using us as one of the fingers on His hand." All these things seemed to be indicators of being on the right path toward the treasure that is ours when we believe. Lead us on, Lord; lead us into your throne room of Grace. Help us to enter into Your presence **boldly** as You instructed this morning in my reading of Hebrews 4:16.

BOLDLY…I thought about that word. What does it mean? Perhaps **B**eholding **O**nly the **L**ord and **D**enying **L**iving for

Yourself. Was the **X** on the treasure map right there in Your Word **BOLDLY** from early this morning? (Hebrews 4:16) I believe it was. You drew the **X** there! Didn't You? You knew You would be found in that word! You were saying, "Here I am," And again in a whisper, "Here I am."

It seems our Savior is not so elusive after all; He is specific. He is trying to make it clear, explaining that, "…only we who believe can enter His place of rest." **X** marks the spot deep in our very own hearts where our Heavenly Treasure, Christ, dwells. When we behold Him and live for Him and not just for ourselves, we will know He is with us. We don't have to go *far* to find our Savior, but sometimes we have to *dig deep* to realize He is already truly buried *within* us! C. G Trumbull wrote that Christ *in* us is a literal, actual, blessed fact, and not a figure of speech. Amen to that!

Mission accomplished… **S**earching **A**nd **N**oticing the **D**ivine today begins and ends by digging for treasure that's buried deep in the heart of every believer, Christ Himself!

4

The Lake

We wait…and we wait…and we wait…wondering. Is God going to show up in our pain? The trials of this life can weigh so heavily. We need some relief! But where will we find it? Will God show up in our struggles, helping us to know He truly never leaves us nor forsakes us?

This day in the *sand* (literally) takes us to a lake. My friend had gone there as a welcome relief from a very troubling time in her life. She needed a change of scenery and a renewed spirit within. Upon arriving at the lake with her friends, she spotted the jet skies for rent. She knew immediately, and voiced it as well, that riding a jet ski was on her personal agenda for the day. Little did she know how very much God had it on her agenda, too!

As she and her friends found a place by the lake to relax and have some fun, disappointment started to settle in…they were far, far away from where the jet skies were available. It seemed her heart's desire was out of reach. And then, out of nowhere, a young man was coming closer…not on land, but on water, and on a jet ski! She and her friends started to notice him and wondered: What was he was doing? Was he some sort of lake patrol? Were they doing something wrong? No. He was just out searching for a cigarette. He asked if anyone had one? And then the thought came to my friend - a cigarette for a ride. What a deal that would be! The whole group was excited to help her with the exchange, anxious to see her wish fulfilled. But she took it upon herself to see if this would be possible. She approached the young man, thus opening up the avenue to receive God's hand of blessing.

The Lake

The young man on the jet ski was happy to honor her request, and even let my friend drive! It was just what the "doctor" ordered to lift the heavy spirit that had been plaguing her of late. While on the ride, the young man mentioned his mother, after all, it was Mother's Day. He was missing his mom, and my friend offered to be his mom for the day. It seems God's intentions were to bless him in the way he most needed it as well.

Where and how does God meet us when we need Him most? The answer is anywhere and in any way that will best meet our needs. Jesus met His disciples along the shore in John 21 also: At dawn Jesus was standing on the beach. (4) "Bring some of the fish you've just caught." (10) "Now come and have some breakfast!" Jesus said. (12)

Does a cigarette help a young man? No. But the comfort of a person offering him God's love can surely be a great blessing. And can a jet ski heal what ails us? Not fully, but it can help a hurting heart to find some healing, knowing that God's love for us is so great He will meet us beside a lake with a bit of nourishment for our souls, just as Jesus did with his friends.

When **S**earching **A**nd **N**oticing the **D**ivine, we can still witness friends of Jesus still getting special treatment today!

5

The Simple Things

My Dad started showing signs of Parkinson's by the age of 60. He has done extremely well, considering the difficulties of the disease. Now he also suffers from fluctuating blood pressure which causes him to black out frequently. Life, for all of us, has many challenges. Through it all, we can see the Hand of God in the situations that come our way—like the other day in a parking lot when my Dad's blood pressure dropped and he once again fell to the pavement. Quickly, a man scooped him up and placed him back in the car. My Mom said it was like he was picking up a rag doll with no effort at all. *Then Peter took the lame man by the right hand and helped him up.* (Acts 3:7) My Dad was not healed in that moment, as the lame man was in Acts, but Dad knows that one day complete healing *will* come.

Dad turned 78 years old recently. I called to wish him a Happy Birthday! He was having a good day. He and my Mom had just gotten home from a drive to one of their favorite spots near Monterey. They had gone there for a picnic. I called just as they were arriving home for their afternoon nap. That's the kind of day you want when you are 78…a fun day followed by a nap! What else is needed? Well, obviously God knows what else is needed.

The night before my Dad's birthday, my parent's neighbor came over and rang their doorbell. He was delivering some freshly cut rhubarb from his garden. Did the neighbor know that rhubarb pie was my Dad's favorite pie? No, he didn't. Did he know that the next day was my Dad's birthday? No, he didn't. But God did! The timing of the delivery of fresh rhubarb was a gift from a God who loves us down to the minutest detail! Fresh rhubarb makes the best pie!

The Simple Things

Recently during a particularly difficult time health wise in my Dad's life, not knowing which way things may go, my Dad said this: "Dying is not a problem. It is an opportunity." When we look at life, and death, as opportunities to witness God's goodness in this life, and in our Heavenly life to come, it can get us through anything.

God used the kindness of a stranger in a parking lot, the thoughtfulness of a neighbor with a gift from his garden, and the delicious pie-making skills of my Mom to deliver *His* love in very special ways to my Dad. Sometimes it's the simple things that mean the most!

When **S**earching **A**nd **N**oticing the **D**ivine, pay particularly close attention to what you're in need of, because God knows what it is, and *He* may soon be delivering it to you!

We love, because he first loved us.
1 John 4:19 (NIV)

6

It's All Good

What's one of the hardest things in life we have to do? Saying good-bye to someone we love tops many lists. And what's one of the hardest things we have to do after we have done that? Say good-bye to the things they wore, loved, and cherished in this life. It seems so wrong and so disrespectful. Shouldn't we just hold onto everything they loved so that we can somehow hold onto them? That's a tough question…

I remember the day I was totally distraught after our son had gone Home to Heaven. I was literally on the floor, sobbing, when it seemed God gently whispered to me, "Go into Phil's room and clean out his dresser." What?!! Could there be a worse time to do something like that? But, God knew best. He knew I was already at such a low point in my grief that nothing could really make it any worse. I obliged God's request, got some bags, and started in…drawer by painful drawer until I was finished. I then placed the bags on the front porch to be picked up the following morning, thankful that I would be at work and not home watching that part of Phil leave me forever. It is a moment in time I will never forget, but will always be grateful for. It had to be done…and I knew I was the one who needed to do it. God helped me make it through.

God shows up in our greatest needs, in our greatest pain, and in our saying "good-bye," as He did for my friend, Lynn, recently. Lynn had taken a trip to San Diego to visit her children and grandchildren, and arrived home to find her husband, Larry, in the backyard. Suddenly, Larry heard the sound of an airplane overhead, and he said, "That's Brian's plane." Brian was Larry's brother, who recently lost his battle with cancer. Brian had a prized airplane that meant the world to him. A biplane, beautiful cream in color, and lovingly cared for. It was the last of what the family needed to sell that once belonged to Brian. It wasn't an easy sell, but the day had come, and seemingly gone, and my friend Lynn was sad to have missed one last chance to see Brian's plane. It was her understanding that the plane had already been picked up by the buyer.

If Lynn had arrived home from San Diego five minutes earlier or later, she would not have been there with Larry in the backyard…he may have told her about Brian's plane having just flown over, and her heart would have yearned to have been there to see it. But God, in all His goodness, knew what it meant for Lynn to see the plane one last time. It turns out the person who bought the plane is from Colorado. His trip to pick it up in California was delayed a few days because of weather. He needed clear skies to fly it home.

As Larry and Lynn stood under those clear skies watching it fly over, they remembered the joy it brought to Brian, and the joy Brian brought to them. Together they watched it until it was lost in the distance…

Lynn's heart was full in that moment as the thought came, "It's all good. There goes Brian." It seemed God was gently whispering to her, "I don't want you to worry about Brian."

We often hope for that one last glimpse of what's been lost. When **S**earching **A**nd **N**oticing the **D**ivine, sometimes we are given just that by our wonderful God.

Whatever is good and perfect
comes to us from God above…
James 1:17a (NLT)

7

Looking Back

Most times we are urged to look forward, to keep moving ahead, one step at a time. But many times we learn so much by taking just a moment to look back. Sometimes we can miss what God is doing in the heat of the moment. It can be easier to **S**earch **A**nd **N**oticing the **D**ivine with hindsight.

I recently spent a few days away with friends. Most times, it's totally fun, and totally relaxing. This time away was a bit different. Some things in life had to be dealt with, and life can be hard stuff. Although this was not a planned getaway, five friends gathered very quickly to say, "I'm in!" That's a miracle in itself in this crazy, busy world.

We made our way to the mountain top to join together about "valley" happenings. Conversations flowed, feelings were expressed, tears were shed, prayers were said, support was given, and what could have become chaos in this world became blessings in God's world. What could have become division became unity. What could have become anger became relief. And only upon looking back, can we see what God so clearly did. He brought friends together to do what friends are meant to do, be there for each other.

We all entered into this time away with different needs. One was dealing with sadness after having to say good-bye to someone. One was needing rest after a job well done. One was filled with confusion and needing clarity. One was feeling alone and needing support. And one was willing to provide the place and the wisdom needed for God's work to be done. It became so obvious on the mountain that God never intended for us to do this life alone. Jesus is the Head, we are the body, and we are to live joined together for good reason! *My flesh and my heart may fail, but God is the strength of my heart and my portion forever.* Psalm 73:26 (NIV)

When we come together with willing hearts in the life of faith, to love God and to love others right where they are at, God's plan works! God's hand is so mighty and so powerful that He can push away any darkness there is and reveal His great light! We came down from the mountain lighter and more ready to run in this race called life. Looking back, we can see God's perfect orchestration of each event. Our faith has been strengthened after watching God meet each specific need in such a miraculous way.

When **S**earching **A**nd **N**oticing the **D**ivine, sometimes we'll be more aware of God after He has just passed by.

> *As my glorious presence passes by,*
> *I will hide you in the crevice of the rock*
> *and cover you with my hand until I have passed by.*
> Exodus 33:22 (NLT)

8

What Have We Missed?

Recently I visited with my longtime friend, Cheryl. We hadn't spent any time together in about three years, and yet we only live an hour and a half apart. Why hadn't we made the effort to connect, to meet face-to-face? We didn't really know why. Was it the busyness of life? Perhaps. Or maybe it was just the effort it takes to set a date that worked for both of us, and follow-through on it. Regardless, it finally happened, and we had a super time together discussing all the things that had transpired since we last met.

During our time together, we talked about our families, our feelings, and our God. We talked about everything two friends could possibly think to talk about, **trying** to catch up on all that we had missed out on. *Trying*…but do we actually have the opportunity to recapture all the experiences that we *could have* been enjoying together, or are they lost? And what is it that's been lost? We probably have no way of knowing. It reminds me of the story of the person who arrives in Heaven and he sees a room full of unopened gifts. He wonders what they are, and he is told that those are all the things God wanted to give him but he never asked for.

When good friends come back together, it is like no time has passed. The reconnection is always there, as it is when we reconnect with God. God never goes anywhere. We can let long periods of time elapse between meetings with our Savior one on one…but how sad is that? I know there are unopened gifts God meant for my friend and me to enjoy together, just as there are many things that go unknown in our relationship with God if we let too much time go by between our talks. Wonderful surprises and experiences are missed because of simple neglect. Really!

God is our Friend. God deserves our faithfulness. After all, "...we were restored to friendship with God by the death of his Son." Romans 5:10

Have I been faithful to my friend of many years? Well, if you had asked me if Cheryl is my friend, I would have said, "Yes." Just as if you ask me if God is my Friend, I would say, "Yes." But am I always faithful in my relationships with both of them? The answer would have to be, "No." I don't always spend the time and energy to stay as close as I should, and I miss out. We all do. But when we do reconnect, it can remind us of what we don't want to continue to miss out on, because it is so good—so TRULY SPECIAL!

When **S**earching **A**nd **N**oticing the **D**ivine, we have to make an *effort*! We have to **actively** stay in close contact with our Friend in Heaven so as not to miss out on what He wants to share with us every day on this earth.

9

Intermingled

Driving to work this morning, I looked at the beautiful trees that lined the street. I looked at the people jogging along the peaceful winding path next to the road. And I thought about Hell. What? You might be thinking…you thought about Hell? Why? I'll tell you why. It's because, sometimes, life can be difficult. It feels like we are living through Hell on earth. This very earth that God designed for us intermingles great beauty with terrible ugliness…**every** day. Because of that, our thoughts about life on earth can get very distorted in thinking *this* is Hell. But this is NOT Hell. This is not even close to Hell. And this is also NOT Heaven. This is not even close to Heaven. What this is, is a fallen world where the good and evil coexist with each other.

Take your hands and put them out in front of you. Now intertwine your fingers and fold them together like you're saying a prayer. Think of your fingers as representing good and evil. Think of each finger as a day, or perhaps a year, or maybe even a season of your life. Now go ahead, wiggle them. One good finger, one bad finger, back and forth we go…and such is life. Why do bad things happen? Well, why do good things happen? If we ask the first question, we need to ask the second. But we don't really hold the answer to either, do we.

Recently, I read a book on a woman who experienced Heaven. And a while back, I read a book about a man who experienced Hell. I started to think of the two extreme opposite experiences they had. The Hell experience was beyond bad! It was devoid of God. There was no love there…no peace…no companionship. But there was lots of pain!! The Heaven experience was FULL of God. It was beyond good! It was filled with Love because God *is* Love.

Intermingled

There's total peace in Heaven…total forgiveness. And there's not a bit of pain…not even the pain of missing those left behind on earth!

And what about present day earth? It's a mixture of both. It is said that this is as close to Hell as some will ever get, and as close to Heaven as some will ever get. But right now, we all get a taste of both. One "tastes" very, very good, and one is quite unacceptable. We want to spit it out!! But we can't have all of God just yet, and we also don't have to endure all of Satan either. One day we will, but not yet. God is giving us time to decide. Why would we not choose the sweetness of a loving God over the distastefulness of Satan?

When Searching And Noticing the Divine in our day, God is helping us see how very good He is, compared to how very evil our enemy is. God is making it **very** clear! God also wants us to know that one day good and evil will no longer intermingle. There will be a great chasm between the two. If we pull our folded hands apart and look at them…we have to ask ourselves a question. Are we choosing to live in the *Right Hand* for all of eternity by saying "Yes" to Jesus today? Because *He will place the sheep at his right hand and the goats at his left.* Matthew 25:33 (NLT), the choice is ours. I pray you'll choose the sweetness of our Heavenly Father.

10

Why Wait?

Waiting…it's not much fun at all. But if we have prayed a lot of prayers, we have probably found out that "Wait" is most often God's immediate answer to us. We shouldn't be surprised by it, but we are. We usually wonder why we have to wait?! Can't it just happen NOW! Most times, God's "Yes" or "No" comes later.

We prayed for years that our son would be healed from Leukemia. We were definitely in waiting mode, and then our answer came on November 14, 2001. The answer was "No." There would be no earthly healing for our child, but there would be a Heavenly one. It's not the answer we would have liked, but it was one that Phil asked for. On his last evening here on earth, Phil said, "I don't want to do this anymore." He said, "It's too hard." Phil asked me if we could ask God. We did…he only waited three hours and then Phil got a "Yes" answer from God. For him there was no more pain, and no more tears!

Some prayers answered with a "Wait" are answered "Yes"! Just this last year, our oldest son waited for an answer at his work. He had requested a raise. It seemed the answer was a strong, "No!" It was very disappointing for him and his wife as he tries to support his family of five on one income. We wanted to be encouraging in the process, but it was hard to watch him in his struggle thinking God's answer was "No." Then, when it was least expected, our son got called into the VP's office. Not only would the raise be given, it was more than he had expected, and it came with a promotion! God had given His *final answer*. It was an emphatic, "YES!" We just had to wait for it!

Why Wait?

Usually there is a good reason why we have to wait for the answer, even if we don't understand. After moving out of our RV recently, and needing furniture for every room, I couldn't understand why the last piece we needed, a headboard, was so hard to find. God had provided everything else so easily. I searched and prayed, and then the day came when it seemed I had found what might work. On a dark, rainy night, when we would have rather stayed home, we took our very large truck out to look at the headboard. We were trying to keep the batteries charged while searching for a buyer. It had towed our RV. When we arrived at the home where the headboard was located, we were met by the owner. As we climbed down out of our huge truck, he asked if we were there for the headboard? And then he said, "I've been looking for a truck just like this to buy." Long story short, we bought his headboard, and the very next night, he bought our difficult-to-sell truck!! God had a great purpose in mind while waiting for our headboard.

When Searching And Noticing the Divine, waiting is not easy most times. But when God's answer does come, we can trust that He has a good reason for everything He does.

In the morning, Lord, you hear my voice;
in the morning I lay my requests before
you and wait expectantly.
Psalm 5:3 (NIV)

11

An Open Wound

This morning, while having my hard-boiled egg with salt and pepper, I remembered a story my friend told me a few years back. Why would my breakfast bring this story to mind? Well, I have a wound on the tip of my finger. Sometimes when cutting hair, the scissors get our fingers instead of our client's hair. That happened to me just the other day, and I have a fresh wound. Fresh wounds do not take well to salt, so I was being protective of my finger tip which brought to mind this story:

My friend and her husband were traveling up the coast of Oregon. It was a beautiful trip because of the combination of redwoods and ocean cliffs! They had stopped along the way and were exploring the beach, when her husband slipped somehow and cut his foot quite severely on the rocks; I believe bone might have even been showing it was such a deep cut!

The most logical thing to do next would have been to make their way back to their car and find the nearest Emergency Room. But this is not what happened. Her husband walked toward the water…toward the SALT water, and he put his foot into the water! YOUCH! That was my thinking when she told me this story. But what happened next was truly a miracle! When the water receded, and he once again could see the cut on his foot, the cut was GONE! Yes! GONE! Completely healed!

So he (Naaman) went down and dipped himself in the Jordan seven times, as the man of God had told him, and his flesh was restored…
2 Kings 5:14 (NIV)

An Open Wound

My friend's husband didn't have to dip seven times. He wasn't instructed to do so. But somewhere in their inner thoughts, by the power of the Holy Spirit, he was directed towards the salt water and not away from it. He was directed towards what could have hurt his open wound tremendously, instead of going to an Emergency Room for help. What seems ridiculous to the human mind, healed my friend's husband instantly by the power of an "unseen" God!

Not all wounds will be healed instantly in salt water along the seashore. In fact, most wounds will **STING** if we try such a thing! I didn't even want salt to touch the small cut on my finger this morning. But, by listening closely to our "unseen" God, we will **SEE** many things that cannot be explained in human terms. If we walk in the direction given to us from the Heavenly realms, it will bring those Heavenly realms into our earthly ones, and we will be astounded at all that is possible with God. When God says, "Walk this way." Let's do it!

Searching **A**nd **N**oticing the **D**ivine will help us see that God is everywhere, and sometimes even showing Himself to us in miraculous ways!

12

Searching the Scriptures

Are we **S**earching **A**nd **N**oticing the **D**ivine on Sunday morning during our church services? Are we really listening, checking what our pastors are saying against Scripture like the Bereans were doing? The Bereans "**searched** the Scriptures day after day to **check up** on Paul and Silas, to see if they were really teaching the truth." (Acts 17:11 NLT)

We might think we are "safe" in church, but listening intently to the teaching we are given, and making sure it lines up with what we read in our Bibles is a must. Being in the Word daily, knowing what it says, helps to safeguard us against being led astray by anyone, anywhere, at any time!

Recently, I was listening to a well known pastor. He was giving a great sermon, and then he said something that made me question him. What was that he just said? Is that right? I even asked my friend who had heard the same sermon online. She said she, too, had questioned that one statement. Let's see if you know the right answer:

Who was it that anointed Jesus with perfume and her hair?

Was it #1 – Mary, the sister of Lazarus and Martha?
Was it # 2 – A woman in the city, which was a sinner?

I had an idea of who I thought it was, and my friend agreed with me, but the pastor mentioned a different person. There was only one thing to do; SEARCH the Scriptures to check up on this pastor!

This search also took me to this site:
http://www.tektonics.org/af/femanoint.html
Take a look at it yourself, if you'd like to find out who it was. It lines this question up against Scripture. It has to. Even the internet gets things wrong!

The answer to this "dilemma" is not really what's most important here. What's most important is that we all need to be like those in Berea. We can't just ride along on the coattails of our pastors, or anyone else who is teaching us the Word of God. We need to be sure we know the Truth when we hear it **and** identify the lies when we hear them. Then we won't be easy prey for our enemy the devil!

> *Be alert and of sober mind. Your enemy*
> *the devil prowls around like a roaring lion*
> *looking for someone to devour.*
> 1 Peter 5:8 (NIV)

13

I'm Going Home!

Remember in childhood when we would be playing a game, and someone wanted to join in with us...and we wouldn't let them? Say it was a basketball game. What would their reaction have been? Perhaps, "I'm taking my ball, and I'm going home then!" Well, we wouldn't have cared. We knew we could just get our own "basketball." We knew we didn't need them, to play *our* game! But what if it's not a simple game of basketball, it's the game of Eternal Life? What if God wants to join in and we won't let Him. What are we left with?

This writing comes from a recent conversation with friends about just such an analogy after hearing Bill Weise, author of, "23 Minutes in Hell," speak. After writing about Heaven and Hell a few weeks back, we actually then had the opportunity of hearing Bill speak in person about his experience in Hell. He was visiting a small church near us, so we decided to go. I want to share with you what our friend, Jack, had to say in our discussions after church.

Jack is a very intelligent, successful, and handsome man, I might add! He lives a good life, with his good wife, who is also my good friend! As we listened to Bill speak, Jack was taking it in, and this is what Jack shared with us. He said he had never really thought about what life would be like with God *completely* removed from the picture. Jack's thinking had been that if a person doesn't spend a lot of time with God, then would God really be missed if eternity was not spent with Him? It didn't seem to be that big of a deal. Perhaps we could function just fine on our own. But, after hearing Bill describe all that Hell *didn't* contain because God was *not* there, Jack got a new perspective on what living *with or without* God would look like. Here's pretty much what Jack said:

I'm Going Home!

*If our eternal life is a game of basketball, and God is not invited to be a part of it, then God not only goes away and takes his ball with Him, but everything else goes with God too…the court, the basket, the friends, the fun, the light, the water, the strength to play, the very air we breathe. And the list goes on. There **is** no game!*

I have thought a lot about this conversation in the weeks since. I have thought about how much is provided for us during our days here on earth, as God's creations. Our Father watches over us, cares for us, nurtures us, and loves us…much like a good parent would. As of now, both those that believe in Him as Lord of their life, and those that don't, are benefiting from God's wonderful presence. In eternity, only those who call Him Lord will live with Him. We all want to be **there** together, on the same Heavenly team!

When **S**earching **A**nd **N**oticing the **D**ivine today, let's give thanks to the Lord, for He is good. He brings so much more to this "game of life" than we give Him credit for!

Whoever has the Son has life;
whoever does not have the
Son of God does not have life.
1 John 5:12 (NIV)

14

Blessings

Blessings come from God. But God uses His people, most times, to pass them along. A friend of mine recently turned 60! To celebrate, she put out a request. She wanted all those who knew her, to *pay it forward*...to do something nice for someone in honor of her birthday, and then let her know. She longed to hear at least 60 nice things that had been done for others in this world. When I had lunch with her the other day, she was well on her way to the 60 blessings from God, through others!

This brought to mind a blessing that came to our family close to 30 years ago. Our boys were very young, and our budget was very tight. One day, while playing out in front of the apartment building where we lived in Alameda, our oldest son found a $20 bill in a bush! We all remember that day very well as a family! Why? Because, the $20 blessed us all with a trip into San Francisco on BART, and a tasty ice cream treat. That would have been unheard of considering our income at that time. Today such a trip would cost at least $75 for a family of five!

In reliving this story once again, tonight during a phone conversation with our son, Jimm, he enlightened us with what he remembered from that day. He said he couldn't be sure, but he remembers finding the $20 bill, and then looking around to see who it might belong to. If his memory is correct, he said there was an older lady standing quite far off in the distance watching him. Jimm always wondered if she had put it there for someone to find...and maybe she even had our boys in mind when she placed it there. God, who of course knew our financial struggles during those years, may have used her to bless us all!

Jimm reminded us that we had asked him what he'd like to do with the money…take a trip to the toy store, or share it with all of us by using it for a trip into San Francisco for ice cream? He chose the city for ice cream. I believe because of that, we *all* remember the $20 gift that day. Jimm was paying it forward, by sharing his blessing with all of us. If he had chosen a personal toy on that day, I wonder, would we all still remember this blessing?

The Bible says, *You should remember the words of the Lord Jesus: "It is more blessed to give than to receive."* We've all heard that quote many times, even if we haven't heard much else in God's Word. It is so true that it feels so good to "get," but it feels even better yet to "give."

When **S**earching **A**nd **N**oticing the **D**ivine today, let's be a part of helping those who are *searching* for God, to find Him. Let's allow God to work through us to bless others. It could very well be a day that will be *noticed* for the rest of their lives!

15

Ready! Set! Go!

About 15 years ago, I learned to ride my bike! You may think it was a little late, in my 40's, to be learning something like that, but it's true. It's not that I hadn't ridden a bike as a child; it's just that I had never ridden a bike quite like I did with *Team In Training*. What started out as a six-mile bike ride that left me thinking that was quite enough for one day, worked its way into riding 100 miles in one day. The goal was to raise money for The Leukemia & Lymphoma Society. The plan was to train for five months to be able to do it. The end result was accomplished…not only once, but twice! It was amazingly difficult, but wonderful!

When riding up very long, very steep hills, I would repeat Philippians 4:13, "I can do everything through Christ, who gives me strength." The hills eventually became my friend, and the flat ground actually became boring. I loved the challenge of the climb, and the soaring down the other side at 35 miles an hour! I did have an incident on my first Century ride that I will never forget. A bungee cord that had been secured to the back of my bike came loose. It tangled itself in the gears of my bike, bringing the back tire to a sudden and complete stop! Smoke could be seen coming from my back tire as the road wore through to the tube, leaving me with a flat tire. I think my snow skiing skills, and lots of prayers from others, saved me on that day as I skidded to a stop! It was truly a miracle that I didn't go flying off my bike! But, without much delay, my tire was fixed, and my ride continued to the finish line. How does one go from riding a mere six miles, and feeling it is enough, to riding 100 miles in a day, five months later?…by spending a lot of time riding and with a lot of encouragement from coaches along the way.

Ready! Set! Go!

As I think about that experience this morning, I think about Jesus' parting words to His disciples; they were not to leave Jerusalem until the gift from His Father was given to them. What gift? The Holy Spirit…their *Coach*…our Coach to this day. In the beginning, we don't recognize the Holy Spirit's voice, or His instructions. It all seems a bit foreign to us. But through the years, the Holy Spirit can become *very* familiar to us if we will do our training "rides" as we should—by spending time in prayer, and in the Word.

Riding 100 miles in a day means taking a simple thing we learned as a child, and doing it a whole new way as an adult. *Jesus loves me this I know, for the Bible tells me so*…but do I know the Holy Spirit? I never realized I could *know* bike riding so well. As believers, may we all say the same thing about knowing the Holy Spirit!

When **S**earching **A**nd **N**oticing the **D**ivine, it is SO important to not leave our "Jerusalem," ie: our homes in the morning, without seeking our *Coach's* advice. We never know when we are going to blow a *tire* in the course of our day. But we can know Who will be there to help us if we do!

> *"Do not leave Jerusalem until the Father*
> *sends you the gift he promised...*
> Acts 1:4 (NLT)

16

A GRAND-Parent's Love

Rising this morning, I read in 2 Thessalonians how Paul started his letter to the people in Thessalonica. It read, "May God our Father and the Lord Jesus Christ give you grace and peace." *Grace* and *Peace* – so needed in our daily walk with God. Grace, to let us know that our sins are covered with Jesus' love. Peace, to fill our hearts full of His love throughout our day.

In thinking about God's love, and a Grandparent's love…it seems they are similar in many ways. So forgiving, so accepting, so much fun! In 2 Thessalonians, Paul wrote, "we always thank God for you…we proudly tell…and God will provide rest for you…"

When we think about our grandchildren, we are so *thankful* for them, so *proud* of them, and ready to *provide rest* for them. God feels the same about us. Parents, on the other hand, need to do their "job." I did mine as a parent. I was instructive, strict, and busy! I'm not saying my children didn't receive love, but it was very different than the love I offer to my grandchildren. I had three boys to raise! I wanted them to be everything they could be, and I am so proud of them today! But with grandchildren, the intention is different. The intention is to love them, and to love them, and to love them. To let them know that their mistakes, their failures, and even their "messiness" is not a problem. When having breakfast with our granddaughter, Kylie, age 8, she spilled an entire glass of orange juice! As a parent I would have reacted differently. But as a grandparent, I can calmly clean up the mess, tell her it's okay, and help her get into new clothes - letting her know she is loved and forgiven instantly…because there is nothing more important in the moments we are with our grandchildren, than those very moments we are with them.

Believe me, I have changed. Our family likes to remember the Bill Cosby routine where he wonders who his mother has become now that she is a Grandma. He says, "This is not the same woman I grew up with! This is an old woman trying to get into Heaven now." That's me! My boys roll their eyes when I squirt whipped cream into their children's mouths, or quickly scoop them up when they are crying to comfort them, or spoil them in a hundred different ways. Our job is to spoil, and to enjoy. Our job is to be proud and tell everyone how adorable our grandchildren are. It doesn't matter the "offense." We forgive, we hug, and we encourage!

While **S**earching **A**nd **N**oticing the **D**ivine today, maybe slipping our thoughts about our Heavenly Father into a **Grand**-Father roll will help us truly receive the grace and peace that Paul wrote about. Let's not be so hard on ourselves! God's love is amazingly patient. Our Father is the **same** yesterday, today and forever. And our **Grand**-Father isn't just *trying* to get into Heaven…He's *already* there!!

> *In the year that King Uzziah died,*
> *I saw the Lord, high and exalted,*
> *seated on a throne; and the train*
> *of his robe filled the temple.*
> Isaiah 6:1 (NIV)

17

She said, "No!"

Have you ever been tempted? What kind of a question is that? Of course, we all have. Well, I want to tell you a story about a friend of mine that simply amazed me with the simplicity and clarity in which God speaks to our hearts, "if" we are listening! I will try to be very sensitive to the nature of this story...

My friend, who I will call, "Mary," lives in a foreign country. She moved back to her homeland for a bit. Her husband presently lives in the states, not yet able to leave his job. Mary LOVES to dance. She told me she loves to dance, the way I love chocolate! That's a big love. One night, recently, she was out in a pub with friends, and there was a lot of dancing going on. There was an old school friend there who I will call, "Bob." Bob also loves to dance, so they danced together all night long, and Mary was having so much fun! As the night wore on, there was a large flow of alcohol, and emotions started to run high. Bob suggested they move to a new pub to dance some more, so they did. Big mistake! Mary said she should never have moved on to a new place with someone who was not her husband.

I know I don't need to fill in all the details of their conversation, but let's just say it included some enticing offers. You see, Bob was recently divorced, and it seemed he was trying to fill a huge hole in his heart with Mary, instead of searching for God in his pain. Bob had been the one to introduce Mary to his church when she moved back home. Yes, they are both believers. But Bob hadn't been going to church since his divorce.

At the end of the night, or should I say early morning hours, it was time to go home. But to whose home would they go? Bob and

She Said, "NO"

Mary walked along, as she pushed her bike. (Very European) When they got to Bob's door, he asked Mary in. Mary said, "No." She told Bob she could not join him out of respect for her husband. And she continued on home. But Mary was floating. It felt like love. It had been such fun! Should she text him? Should she call him? She did neither. The next day a simple question from her sister brought her back to her senses. Her sister asked, "Did Bob walk you home?" Mary said, "No." It was then that a light went on in the darkness! Bob had not even cared enough to keep her safe in the wee hours of the night. When Mary did see Bob on the street a few days later, they casually greeted one another, and went on their way. Oh, how the enemy could have lured them into his trap, and turned Mary's whole world upside down! Thankfully, her walk with Christ was stronger than her walk home to Bob's door!

When **S**earching **A**nd **N**oticing the **D**ivine, let's always notice who it is we are walking with. God will surely lead us safely home; the enemy will only lead us to his trap!

Do not let sin control the way you live;
do not give in to its lustful desires.
Romans 6:12 (NLT)

18

Divine Moments

School recently started here in the San Francisco Bay Area, as it has around the rest of the country. Moms are happy, the kids are sort of happy, and the grandparents...well, we just get to have fun with it all. I did, as I took each of my grandchildren who live close by out for ice cream as a special treat to celebrate. Not to mention, I get ice cream three times! The calories aren't what I need, but it surely is enjoyable with the kiddos!

During these times, there have been Divine moments with the young ones! God keeps showing up! Laila, age five, just started kindergarten. We went to my house, per her request, and read together after ice cream. We read the children's Bible I keep here. We turned to a story of Joseph, and read how he was a brave and honest man. I asked Laila if she knew what "honest" meant? She then admitted to me that sometimes she lies a little. But she tries not to. When I took her home that day, as she was getting out of the car, she said to me, "I'm gonna tell Mama that I forgot my headband at school." She was on a mission of honesty. Her Mama accepted the message well, and commended her for telling the truth! We had not planned this "lesson." But God had, because Laila had recently gotten into a bit of trouble for not telling the truth.

Then came the day of ice cream with Jackson, age seven. Back to the ice cream shop, where Jackson got his favorite flavor, chocolate. We sat outside in the warm sun to eat it. I'm sure you can imagine the chocolate mess that was spread all over his hands and face! But where was he to wash up? With no bathroom in sight, I instructed him to start licking!! Then all of a sudden, he lit up! I hadn't heard it, but he had! The sprinklers turned on! He knew immediately that water had been provided to wash in. Then we were on our way to our next adventure, which was to head to the foothills and get out the binoculars. I told him we were looking for mountain lions. What we saw was even bigger than that! Standing close to the railroad tracks, we looked up and down, and there it came...a large, very real, very LOUD train! When we got back into the car, Jackson said, "This is one of the best days of my life! We were so *lucky*!" I said, "Jack, we were really *blessed* today! God knew we needed water, and He knew we would love to see a train! Do you know how to spell blessed Jack?

B-L-E-S-S-E-D."

Then came the day for grandchild number three to enjoy some ice cream. I arrived at the house to pick up Denell just as my daughter-in-law needed to go get Jack from school. All her daycare kids were asleep, so it was God's perfect timing for me to go get him. Afterwards, I had a wonderful time with Denell, enjoying her choice of frozen yogurt. We chatted. We ate. And we shopped...seeing God's blessings in the details of our day.

When **S**earching **A**nd **N**oticing the **D**ivine together, how many ways can we see God perfectly orchestrating our days? Just as Jack and I were on a hunt, so our hearts should also be *searching* for the Divine and His miraculous provisional moments. It is such fun!

19

Anything?

I love how sitting and talking with friends can reveal the most amazing God stories! If we are listening, God is explaining the way He works through stories. My friend talked the other day of me being a conduit. Maybe that's what writers really are; they listen, they watch, and then they write. We couldn't possibly experience all the things God has for us personally, so He shares them through other people! That's true of this story:

When my friend, Aimee, was in her mid teens, just about 14 or 15, she experienced something that she will never forget. Her mom had arrived home, and after coming into the house, she asked Aimee to go out to the car to get a bag off the back seat. Aimee was not at all happy to oblige her mom's request. After much resistance and arguing, she finally complied. What Aimee found on the back seat was a coat that she had been so wanting! She couldn't have felt happier and worse, all at the same time. Aimee had been resistant to do what her mom asked of her, and her mom only wanted to bless her!

I love hearing this story after reading the book, "Anything," by Jennie Allen. This book challenges us to pray and be willing to do *anything* for God…whatever, whenever He asks. Our Father in Heaven knows our greatest blessings are in our obedience to Him. Why then, are we so resistant to His requests? It seems the more I pray *anything,* the more I want to argue that there might be a better way to go about my Father's business! Maybe that's all part of the growing process…to at least begin to recognize when we are resistant, and become less so through the years? As an adult, Aimee is much more willing to comply to *anything* her mom asks of her. It's not all about what's in it for her now, but what she can do to serve her mom. As we grow in Christ, shouldn't this be our goal?

I've been reading a lot in Philemon lately. It's a very small book in the Bible between Titus and Hebrews. Paul is making a request of his friend, Philemon, on behalf of Onesimus. He writes, "I am praying that you will really put your generosity to work, for in so doing you will come to an understanding of all the good things we can do for Christ." He writes, "You are generous because of your faith." Without faith, this world is all about us, and not really about asking God, "Is there *anything* I can do for You, or Your people today?" It's a bold prayer. But Paul writes, "…I am boldly asking a favor of you." He writes, "I could demand it in the name of Christ because it is the right thing for you to do, but because of our love, I prefer just to ask you." Most times, God gently asks us to do the right thing through a quiet whisper from within.

While **S**earching **A**nd **N**oticing the **D**ivine, we can begin to see that God has blessings waiting for us on the other side of our obedience to His whispers. Paul writes, "I didn't want you to help because you were forced to do it but because you wanted to." The question is, are we willing to grow up enough to want to do *anything* our Father asks?

20

Being Guarded!

Are we being guarded against the strategies and tricks of the devil? We need to be! As our pastor said in a recent sermon, the enemy knows how to deliver Smart Bombs – bombs that know where to go, and just when to explode in our hearts and in our minds! We are in a battle every single day with a very clever foe! Without God's Truth as our protection, we will be an easy target!

We just got back from Oregon, visiting the kids and grandkids! Our eight year old granddaughter, Kylie, and I love to study the Bible together. This time we were reading Philippians 4:6-7. It talks about not worrying about anything, but praying about everything. Usually we worry about most things, and pray about some things. How do we get this so mixed up? It goes on to say, "Tell God what you need, and thank him for all he has done." What happens then? Well, "**If** you do this, you **will** experience God's peace, which is far more wonderful than the human mind can understand." (Bold added) As I read that again this morning, I looked up at the picture on the wall across from where I sit here in the SAND Room…it's a beautiful photo of a hammock in the tropics. It looks like total peace to me. But then I thought, "There's no peace in that hammock if there's no peace in our hearts and minds while we're lying there."

Philippians 4:7 says that, "peace will guard our hearts and minds as you live in Christ Jesus." Funny thing is, when Kylie and I were reading this and discussing it, she did what seemed a very childish thing to do…she not only placed her open Bible on her chest, she then later placed it on her head. But, it was a perfect illustration of what we were studying! I started to shoot pretend arrows at the Bible while it was on her chest - arrows of fear, and worry. I showed Kylie how they bounced right off the Bible and back out into the air. I told her that God's Word was guarding her heart from the arrows the enemy tries to hurt us with. And later when she placed the Bible on her head, it seemed silly at first, but then I realized the opportunity that God was giving me to do the very same thing again. So I shot pretend arrows at Kylie's head, with the arrows bouncing back off into the air, explaining to her that God was now guarding her mind from the attacks of the enemy! What a very simple, but very clear illustration of what God is doing when we are spending time in His Word.

When **S**earching **A**nd **N**oticing the **D**ivine together, sometimes God can use childish things to teach us very grown-up lessons of His love and protection in our lives. The enemy's Smart Bombs are nothing compared to God's Holy Wisdom! Let's use it daily!

21

A Trip Home

Jim and I just returned from a trip home to Fresno. I say "home," because it is where we grew up, met in High School, and married 37 years ago. We were visiting Jim's mom and family this past weekend. She lives within walking distance of the church I attended in High School, and we were married in. We were meeting my brother and his wife there. They recently started attending Northwest Church again. While sitting in the pew, waiting for Steve and Marlene to arrive, a gentleman was making his way down our row from the far end. He stopped in front of us and mentioned something about not coming in this way normally. We chatted just a bit before it became known to us that he was the pastor at Northwest now. We were surprised! We told Pastor Will how we had been married in this church. He ended our conversation by saying we were going to enjoy today's service.

It turned out the service was a Celebration service. Pictures were shown of how the church looked when it started 55 years ago — a little white chapel on the corner. When I first attended there with my family, we were in that little chapel until the present–day church was built just a few years later. In the sermon, Will talked of looking back and looking forward, as they are planning a new church plant in Clovis. He said that Northwest was a church plant out of Kingsburg — something I didn't know. When the service was over, I asked my brother, Steve, if he had met Will yet. He needed to. After all, Steve is practically one of the Founding Fathers! He said he hadn't, so we made our way up afterward to talk with Will. We told him how our whole family had started attending Northwest because of Steve. Steve's buddy, James, had led him to Christ in his Senior year of High School. Steve was looking for a church to go to, and our Dad suggested he try our

A Trip Home

Grandma's church over there on the corner. Steve did, and because he did, our parents did, and the rest is our family's history. Northwest Church, with Bufe Karraker as pastor, changed our family's eternal lives — one and all!

Will was born the very year Steve became a Christian. God knew that one day they would meet, standing under the very same "Old Rugged Cross" of two railroad ties that was hung in the then *new* church building many years ago. Everything else has been remodeled over the years. But the Cross remains the same. This was a *divinely* appointed morning if I've ever seen one! The pastor came down, not the aisle, but our particular row, and stopped and talked to us, of all people. We had not been there for YEARS! When we met with him afterward, we were able to deeply affirm for Will how important church planting is, by sharing our rich family history in this church — and how, generations later, the spiritual benefits from Northwest Church continue on! Steve prayed for Pastor Will before we left that day. It was a day we won't soon forget!

We didn't have to Search far to Notice the Divine today! It was a short walk to the corner church where I met our Savior over 40 years ago. We saw God use us as His vessels – a display of what God will do with a church plant. Everything Will is believing for the future of Northwest Church, could be seen by looking at where its past had brought us.

They will be called oaks of righteousness,
a planting of the Lord for the
display of his splendor.
Isaiah 61:3 (NIV)

22

What Does God Sound Like?

What does God sound like when He speaks to us? Isn't that the age-old question we all want to know the answer to? I can't tell you exactly what God sounds like, but I can tell you what it looks like when we do hear Him and obey Him by sharing this story with all of you. Maybe this will help all of us recognize the sound of God's voice just a bit better.

Our middle son, Chris, has a great job! He is a Journeyman Plumber in San Francisco. If you're going to be in the union, that is the one to be in. It truly helps him support his family of five here in the Bay Area where things are not cheap, I say we pay for our weather here. It's beautiful. But it's costly! Chris was at work on Tuesday, as usual, but something was gnawing at him. His wife, Holly, was headed to a funeral service for her Dad's brother. Chris works hard, and is dedicated. He had recently taken some time off for an illness, and also needed Wednesday off to be at the hospital, where their little five-year old was having tubes put in her ears. He fully planned on working Tuesday, instead of going to the funeral. That is, until the voice of God overrode Chris' plans.

As Chris worked, it seemed like he was in the wrong place. It truly felt that he needed to be with Holly at the funeral. It was a hard call…he knew his boss wasn't going to be too happy. But Chris knew deep inside what he needed to do. After a couple hours of work, he spoke with his boss and explained the situation. His boss didn't want him to leave the job with the pressing deadline they had to meet, but he relented that Chris really did need to go.

When I returned to Chris and Holly's house with their children on that Tuesday, after picking them up from school, Chris was not there, and I wondered why. I thought he would have returned from work by then. I was a bit puzzled as to what had changed. I found out he had gone to the service. When Chris told me later what had happened, and how it had all turned out just the way it was supposed to, I was so proud of him. In fact, I just sent him a message on his phone, this morning. It read, *Loved hearing how God spoke to you about the service on Tuesday. If you wonder what the Holy Spirit sounds like when He is prompting us to do something, that is how. And you listened and were obedient, and it was a great blessing. It makes me so happy to know you hear the voice of God and do what He is asking.*

When **S**earching **A**nd **N**oticing the **D**ivine in our day, we have to remember what we learned in Kindergarten. We have to put our *listening ears* on so we can hear our great Teacher speak to us. We can complicate it if we want to. But when we just listen, and obey, we will get to know what God sounds like. Those steps of faith are rewarded with true contentment.

"Speak, Lord, for your servant is listening."
1 Samuel 3:9 (NIV)

23

One of the Devil's Lies

Having my quiet time in the morning is my favorite time of the day. It didn't used to be. My Bible used to collect dust on the shelf, or be put away in a drawer somewhere. But that doesn't work for me anymore. Life's circumstances, past and present, don't allow for a lazy relationship with God — it needs to be vital and alive and GROWING! But one of the devil's lies I've been hearing a lot lately is, "You really don't need to be reading the Word *again*. You've read it hundreds of times." I have been having tempting thoughts to skip my morning time with God, because the enemy is trying to convince me that there are no huge changes happening — and reading it will probably be a waste of time. But because my morning quiet time is a habit now, I'm able to push through those thoughts. I continue to get my coffee, peel my banana, and go sit with the Word. And do you know what happens? When I keep reading and praying, God *always* rewards that time with His reassuring wisdom! 2 Peter 1:12 said this morning, "I plan to keep on reminding you of these things – even though you already know them, and are standing firm in the truth." That sounds like God speaking directly to the enemy's lie! No wonder the devil doesn't want us in God's Word! He knows his dark lies will be brought into God's revealing light!

In thinking about this struggle, it came to me…it's like our child learning new things. In the beginning, everything is a huge accomplishment! And we get so excited for the growth and maturity we see! It's SO visible, and we share it with everyone! But as adults, we probably don't see huge daily changes in ourselves. It's a good thing, since growing older comes fast enough! As mature Christians, too, most times we probably won't see huge daily changes in our spiritual growth. Because of that, we might think we can skip a daily time with our Father. It might not make that much of a difference after all… But we are being **totally duped** by a very clever enemy. It is a LIE! Strangely, although we might not notice the help we get daily from time in the Word, it is there. How can we know? Because when we **don't** start our day focused on God's ways, our "walk" will not be as intentional towards the things of God. We will be more self-focused than God-focused. We will have remnants of the fruit of the Spirit — love, joy, peace, patience, kindness, goodness, faithfulness, gentleness, and self-control. But we won't have these working to full capacity. I don't know about you, but I want all cylinders firing completely! I want gas in my tank, and the oil filled, because our enemy is ruthless. He will take us down any chance he can get! We must diffuse his lies with the TRUTH!

When **S**earching **A**nd **N**oticing the **D**ivine, it helps to know what we are looking for in our day. We can start by not listening to the enemy, but listening to the Word of God. Once we set our bearings there, the rest of our day will come quite supernaturally!

Submit yourselves, then, to God.
Resist the devil, and he will flee from you.
James 4:7 (NIV)

24

I Saw Jesus Today!

I went to a yard sale this morning. It is not my normal way to spend a Friday morning. In fact, I'm usually at work on Friday and Saturday, so I don't get to yard sale shop when most sales are going on! I was excited to meet with my sister, Karen, and check out this special yard sale I had heard about. I picked her up early, wanting to be there for the best picks.

My sister is a master at not only having yard sales, but shopping at them. I knew I was going with an expert, and I was glad. I wanted to get a good deal on the things we would see, and I knew she would steer me right. I wasn't disappointed. We found some great items, and got some good deals. We then made our way over to the house next door. I guess they decided if one neighbor was going to draw a crowd, why not put it to good use. That's when I saw "Jesus!"

What did He look like? You're not going to believe this...but He looked exactly like Karen! It wasn't the second coming of Christ. But here's what Jesus looks like before His actual return. He looks like someone who finds a few valuable items at a garage sale, and doesn't take advantage of the owners. He looks like someone who kindly explains to a little old lady from Germany what a couple of her books listed at a dollar could really bring. He looks like someone who picks up an old toy and tells this same person that she should really look into how much it would be worth...because it's exactly what the "pickers" would be looking for. It's a generous spirit in a human body!

To be honest, I didn't look as much like Jesus today as my sister did. I was looking for deals. And even when my total purchase only came to $14, I offered $12 instead. We settled on $13. I thought that's how it was done. But, Karen taught me more than how to make a deal today. She showed me what it looks like to "be" Jesus to people even when they don't know that's Who they are seeing. The name of Jesus wasn't even mentioned. But His love was so visible! When we left, the lady said, "Please come back! You're fun!" She knew that most people would have paid the buck or two and turned it into a few hundred. And nobody would blame anyone for doing that. But I have to tell you, as exciting as it would have been to make a couple hundred dollars, it was a lot more exciting to see "Jesus" today — to see His kindness, His generosity, and His way of doing what's right, and not just what's popular and selfishly advantageous.

When **S**earching **A**nd **N**oticing the **D**ivine, we might just see Jesus! We have to have our eyes open and looking for more than a deal. We have to look for a heart like His, in a world that isn't. Little sisters can teach us a thing or two, not only about yard sales, but about Jesus!

The generous will themselves be blessed...
Proverbs 22:9 (NIV)

25

Does God Care About Football?

Does God care about football? I really don't know what God thinks about football. But I do know that God cares about everything, and everyone!! This last weekend was such a sweet example of that. Our son Jimm, and granddaughter Kylie, had driven down from Oregon for just one day. Nine hours down, one day here, and nine hours back again. Why? Because Jimm was joining his brother, Chris, at the Raider game on Sunday. The brothers had gotten season tickets in the black hole as a gift from their brother, Phil 12 years ago, although Phil was not present at the gift giving. He had just gone Home to Heaven a month before Christmas, and we had used some of his life insurance money to purchase the boys Season Tickets that year in remembrance of him. Chris continues to purchase the tickets. We are die-hard Raiders fans!

Jimm has since moved to Oregon. He has three children, so he seldom gets to attend the games anymore. This was a special time for him and Chris. But on Saturday, Chris was in excruciating pain!! After a trip to the ER, he found out he had a kidney stone. It looked like all game plans were off, unless Jimm wanted to go with someone else. He didn't. He said he had come to town to spend time with his brother more than anything else, and he would sit at home with him and watch the game with him if need be. I was so proud of his attitude about it all. These "boys" are now in their 30's, but they are still our boys!

Up until late Saturday night, Chris was on painkillers, but come Sunday morning, it seemed the pain was gone, and the guys were able to head to the game – tailgating and all! They were some of the smart ones who went into the game early enough to see the

Does God Care About Football?

quarterback take the first snap of the drive and run it 93 yards down field for a touchdown – the longest run for a quarterback in NFL history! The guys had a great time at the game. The Raiders even won their first game in ten years after a bye week, and Chris felt fine…until Monday morning. Halfway to work, the pain began again, and Chris ended up driving himself to the ER. It was looking like surgery was needed. They were going to fit him in…so we waited…**ALL DAY**, until at last the surgeon came in about 8:00 P.M. He recommended not doing the surgery. Chris was not so sure, even though the pain had subsided. He didn't want to go home, and have the pain come right back. But Chris agreed to wait and see, spending the night in the hospital. The next morning, plop, plop, fizz, fizz…oh what a relief it is! The stone came out!

The reason why I tell you this entire story is because when **S**earching **A**nd **N**oticing the **D**ivine in our lives, we can see God in so very many ways! We can see Him in our joys and in our sorrows. We can see Him in our best days and in our worst. And we should. We should see God in all things, because He is always with us. Chris will never forget the pain he was in. But he, and all of us, will never forget God's goodness in it all. To have the pain completely gone on Sunday so the brothers could enjoy the game together, watching history be made, was such a huge blessing! We all stand in awe of God's timing. We know that all things are not what seems like perfect timing to us. To have our youngest son leave us at the age of 16 doesn't seem like God's perfect timing. But when we keep our focus on God, and keep our prayers ascending Heavenward, we can witness some very amazing things! Does God care about football? Well, I hope Terrelle Pryor is thanking God for his history making touchdown! What I do know, is that God cares about families, and brothers, and our sons – and this mom's heart is very grateful for all that God does each day!

How we praise God, the Father of our Lord Jesus Christ, who has blessed us with every spiritual blessing in the heavenly realms because we belong to Christ.
Ephesians 1:3 (NLT)

26

Offer Up a Prayer!

Have you ever been running late to an event and needed the perfect parking space? Who hasn't? But how many of us have offered up a prayer for that parking space? Is God even listening when we make such a seemingly silly request? Isn't the world full of much bigger problems for God to be working on? Is it wasting God's time to even ask? Does He mind? Will He answer?

My daughter-in-law, Holly, shared a great story with me today! Holly was finishing up a busy day with her daycare business. I actually happened to be there when her friend came in with her four children, adding to Holly's three children, and about four other daycare children still needing to be picked up. When I left, there was one child still waiting for their parent, and Holly was running behind. She and her friend, Joni, were going to a book signing in San Francisco. They needed to be on the road, but were running late.

Holly and Joni headed to the city, finding their way to the Castro District. It was packed with people. There wasn't a parking space to be had, let alone a clear street to drive down! Cars and people were everywhere! That's when Holly decided to offer up a prayer. Hands gripping the steering wheel, she called out, "Please, God, help us find a parking spot!" Her friend Joni said, "Oh, Holly!" But Holly responded with, "Hey, you've prayed for a lot more frivolous requests! God *will* give us a parking spot!" They soon turned a corner that was practically void of any cars—first unbelievable moment! Then right there, in front of the Castro Theater/book signing location, a van started to pull out of its parking spot—second unbelievable moment...so unbelievable that it brought on the third unbelievable moment. A storekeeper was

Offer Up A Prayer?

out in front of his shop, sweeping up at day's end. Holly asked him if this was *really* a parking spot? He said, "Yes it is! And it's *always* full." Do you want to know what happened then? They got out to put money in the parking meter, and it said, "Free Parking." It seemed God had gone above and beyond the prayer Holly had even asked! Holly and Joni entered the book signing event only a few minutes late—just in time to hear the author start reading from her book!

I believe, with Holly's story, God was putting an exclamation point on the book I am reading right now by Will Stoll, "40 Days of Prayer." Interestingly, I am on Chapter 9, "Getting results – Asking!" We all need to *ask* much more, in Jesus' name. God wants us to. He *asks* us to. We must!

When **S**earching **A**nd **N**oticing the **D**ivine, *asking* is a BIG part of seeing God! Holly and Joni never would have seen God so clearly if Holly had not asked what she did! Holly said it was like God parted the "Sea of Cars" when they turned that corner, and the angels sang out in a Heavenly refrain as the van pulled out of that parking spot. Sometimes it's the little things that show us how very **BIG** God's love is!

Until now you have not asked for anything in My Name. Ask and you will receive, and your joy will be complete.
John 16:24 (NIV)

27

Pray or be Prey!

We all have decisions to make every day. They can be big decisions, or very small ones. But one thing is for sure, there is usually a war going on in our mind about what to do. In Romans, Paul talks about how he wants to do what is right, but he ends up doing what is wrong. He writes, *"...another law at work within me that is at war with my mind."*

I had a decision to make recently. Even though it wasn't a big deal, the decision was. It involved whether I would do what *I wanted to do* with my day, or what *God had in mind*. And it involved my grandchildren, of all people! And I was thinking about myself, my wants...and I knew it. I wanted to be selfish. It was a test of the "Emergency Broadcast System" from Heaven! I knew what the Holy Spirit was asking. And I knew God was watching, and waiting to see if I would put others above myself.

Okay, here was the deal. (You're going to laugh!) Do I go to the pumpkin patch, through the corn maze, etc...or do I stay home in front of the fire, with some good food, and watch the football game on a Sunday afternoon? See, like I said, no "big deal" here. It's not that I didn't want to go...it's that I wanted to be lazy more! But the *Big Deal* was the battle in my mind, because I believe the enemy wanted me to miss out on a very special time with the little ones and my daughter-in-law. The enemy wanted me to be selfish, and to listen to my own desires instead of God's desires for my life. God won this time. The enemy lost. And I am grateful! Most victories don't come without a battle in the mind. *The mind governed by the flesh is death, but the mind governed by the Spirit is life and peace.* Romans 8:6 (NIV)

Pray or be Prey!

I read a devotional recently by Charles Stanley. He talked about time. He said that God will not give us more to do in our day, than the time He gives us to do it. I have been thinking about that a lot. How come we run out of time in our day, seemingly having more to do than the time we have to do it? Charles Stanley says we must then ask ourselves if what we are doing is really God's will, or our own? That's a good daily question. And the funny thing is, when we are *in* God's will, like going to the pumpkin patch, God still makes plenty of time later in the day for the fire, the food, and the recorded football game. I had my "cake and eat it too," so to speak. The whole day can be a complete pleasure when the peace of God is reigning in our hearts and minds…first obedience, then peace.

When **S**earching **A**nd **N**oticing the **D**ivine, we must ask ourselves whose will we are in—God's or our own? We will miss seeing a wonderful Divine plan for each day if we choose our own will over God's. This battle of wills will *always* be with us as long as we live upon this present–day earth because Satan continuously prowls around like a lion, looking for someone to devour!! So, we can either pray and obey, or we can be Satan's prey as we disobey!

28

Thank You, Lord!

Down to the minutest detail!! That's the first thought that came to me as I began to share this story with you. It's not only that God knows us down to the minutest detail, it's that He even cares about all those tiny details! It baffles my mind! Here's what happened...

A good friend invited me to a wonderful Christmas dinner put on by her church. There were beautiful tables set by all the women, each in their own design. There was a raffle, an inspirational speaker, and wonderful fellowship. The evening not only included one of my favorite singers, but also a dessert buffet that would make anyone drool...especially people like me who would always eat dessert before any meal. I LOVE dessert!

Upon arrival, we bought our raffle tickets, met a few of the ladies, and browsed the dessert buffet, wetting our appetites for what we would enjoy later. I quickly spotted the dessert that I would like most! Did I mention that all these desserts were homemade by the women in the church? I was tempted to just take my selection back to the table right then...I mean, why wait? I was here now. I could just save it for after the dinner. But I resisted the "temptation," and quietly and empty-handedly made my way back to my seat.

The dinner began, and so too, the music. Besides dessert, the musical part of the evening was what I was most excited about. But here's what happened. We were one of the very last tables to be served, which meant that when we were just getting our meal, many of the tables were already filing over towards the dessert buffet, and the line got longer and longer and longer! It got so long that it started to wind its way through the middle of the room, with women standing in front of the stage where Staci Frenes had started to sing. As I finished my meal I had a choice to make…do I add to the long line, or do I just sit and enjoy Staci? It seemed best that I just sit, and let the desserts go to whomever. I could live without what I had spotted. It wouldn't be the end of the world…and I wanted to honor Staci by staying seated and giving her my attention. And do you know what God did? He honored me by having the *very* dessert that I had had my eye on *hand delivered* to me by our table hostess. I couldn't believe it! As I sat there thinking, "Someone has to be last in line, I'm choosing to be that person," she walked up to our table with a small sampling of the desserts that she and others had been in line for, and offered me my choice. And there it was—the very dessert I wanted most…a yummy rice crispy treat, flavored with peanut butter, and covered in a thick, chocolate frosting! She had no idea that she was the Hands of God making a delivery. It wasn't just a dessert, but it was the "desire of my heart" dessert that God alone knew about.

Now, you may be thinking, this is such a **small** thing, why do you even share it? Because, when **S**earching **A**nd **N**oticing the **D**ivine each day, this is usually how God shows up. We can see our Father's **HUGE** love for us in so many little ways! In the grand scheme of life, this is nothing. But to God, it *is* something, because He takes pleasure in loving on His children.

I will thank you, Lord, with all my heart;
I will tell of all the marvelous things you have done.
I will be filled with joy because of you.
I will sing praises to your name, O Most High.
Psalm 9:1-2 (NLT)

29

Dedicated to You, Jesus

The SAND Room stories this month will be dedicated to Jesus. I have other stories waiting…wonderful stories that have been shared with me about the Divine showing up in our ordinary days. I love those stories. But for the month of December, I want to talk about Jesus, and Christmas stories. I put a comma there, separating the two for a reason. I have a writing coming out about the controversy of this season. Some will like what I have to say, some will disagree with it, and some might even be confused about it all. Let me just say, I understand there are some "hills to die on," and others not so much. Our eternal life in Heaven based on Jesus Christ is a "hill to die on." When we say, "Yes, to Jesus," we say, "Yes," to all that He came to give us. He is, He was, and He will always be our only way to enter through the gates of Heaven—having been cleansed of our sins by His blood shed on the Cross!

So, why, oh why, do I start with that on this December day? Because, I went Christmas shopping today, and these shopping days can turn into some of the most unholy, rushed, and stress-filled days of the year…and I didn't want it to be like that. Not for one minute! So I drank in, not only my coffee this morning, but the Word of God. Then I got excited to go out and meet the world in the stores today! (Normally, I'm not much of a shopper.) I wanted to be "Jesus" out there to everyone I came in contact with…with that mindset, it seemed I got to see a bit of the world through His eyes. And I have to tell you, it looked good! I saw people making sure they were not cutting in line. I witnessed people being more than courteous in crowded areas, to make room for others. I had the opportunity to give my place in line to a woman who was on her lunch hour and needed to get back to work. I saw someone bump a large stack of pajamas onto the floor, only to have two of us quickly help her restack them on the shelf. We felt her gratitude. I saw smiles, and was helped by patient employees who, when asked, didn't love their job, but had been at it for 12 years and still remained cheerful. Plus, God helped me find gifts for those I love and care about. It seemed everyone was on their best behavior…or was it just my attitude that was on its best behavior? Is that why I saw the best in all people? Is it what's inside of us, or is it what's going on around us, that determines our day? Oh, and I LOVED saying "Merry Christmas" to everyone along the way! Because it is **Christ** who makes us all *merry* when we remember what His birth means to this world! *She will give birth to a son, and you are to give him the name Jesus, because he will save his people from their sins.* Matthew 1:21 (NIV)

In **S**earching **A**nd **N**oticing the **D**ivine today, I chose not to just blend into the hustle and bustle of the season. I chose to go slowly, and love my "neighbor." That's who we are to be in Christ *every day*, not just in December. What a waste of a day it can be if we leave the Divine at home when we venture out into the world that He created for us to enjoy!

30

Oh, Holy Night

Oh, Holy night, and Holy day, and Holy year! May God always be honored and worshiped as He desires to be. That is my heart's desire. But my heart is struggling these days, as we enter into the Christmas season. What does it all mean? Are we really to be celebrating Christmas? It seems not, according to some. And not because some governmental agency wants to take down our display of the Christ child in a manger, but because those who are deeply devoted to God want to. What?...you might be saying. Yes, I say. After years and years of celebrating the birth of our Savior on December 25th, I am hearing more and more about how this is not Jesus' actual birthday, and how He has never asked us to worship Him in this way. It is documented that December 25th started as a pagan holiday way back when, by a Roman Emperor by the name of Aurelian. It was a date set to worship the sun god. It is being claimed that the disciples didn't celebrate any of the holidays we do today...so that being said, we aren't supposed to either. Are we really supposed to cancel Christmas, and Easter, and many other traditions that we, as Americans, celebrate? I guess we can keep Thanksgiving...although that is being debated too, by some.

Where am I going with all of this, if you have continued reading to this point? Some of you are totally agreeing with what I have written so far, some have never heard of this, and some, like me, have heard of it, are hearing of it more, and wonder what to do about it? I mean, we have always gathered with our families, put up a Christmas tree, bought presents for one another, and celebrated Jesus' birth with a big feast! Is there a right and wrong about it? That's what I'm trying to get to the bottom of here.

Here's what's prayerfully coming to me on this day…because I have asked God to stop my fingers from typing if I am not honoring Him by what I am discovering on this journey…and I'm still typing, so take it for what it's worth. The disciples didn't celebrate as we do. Okay, well, they were Jewish, and we are Gentiles, for the most part, so their family traditions would already be different than ours. (We don't celebrate Guy Fawkes Day either, because we aren't English.) Secondly, Jesus hadn't been revealed as the Messiah to them in their growing up years, so when they "met" Him, they wouldn't have exactly been celebrating His birthday. Thirdly, they celebrated many things in their Jewish traditions, which are all wonderful. But when Jesus was born, the wise men did bring Jesus birth-day gifts, and they did worship Him. "Where is the new born king of the Jews? We have seen his star as it arose, and we have come to worship him." Matt. 2:2 (NLT) They are not worshiping a sun god, or even the star; they have come to worship Jesus, the King of the Jews. They "…fell down before him and worshiped him. Then they opened their treasure chests and gave him gifts." Matt 2:11 (NLT) That sounds like a wonderful celebration of Jesus' day of birth to me!

Okay, so we have the date wrong. It is sometime in the spring actually. No one really knows for sure. And this December 25th date was used for some pagan rituals. So, should we just hand it over to the pagan worshipers, or should we take it back, take back *every day* that the Lord has made, since He was the one who made all days in the first place? And should we not also take back His trees, and His mistletoe that He made? The evergreen tree was chosen to represent Christ, because its green leaves were constant and never-changing, like Christ's love. Does Satan just get to keep these things since he took them? Satan is using them wrong, and he didn't make them. Jesus did! "He was in the beginning with God. He created everything there is." John 1:2-3 (NLT) It sort of reminds me of the Grinch, in "The Grinch Who Stole Christmas." When his heart grew three sizes because of the love the Whos showed to him, he gave back everything to Whoville that he had stolen. The Grinch couldn't keep Christmas from coming, because it wasn't about the trinkets he had stolen, it was about love.

Christmas, any day, doesn't belong to the prince of this world, it belongs to the Prince of Peace, Jesus Christ.

Now Santa Claus was, from what I read, originally the god Odin, and eventually became St. Nicholas. Was this right or wrong - bad idea, or good? Well, "The light shines through the darkness and the darkness can never extinguish it." John 1:5 (NLT) I like that we took the "honor" away from the god Odin, and brought it back into the Light of Jesus...His gift-giving spirit!

Have you heard, or did you know, that Christmas has been outlawed in certain countries through the years? England outlawed it in the 1640's. They said because it was directly contrary to Christianity...understandable, when worshiping other gods. But isn't it interesting how today, in America, it is mainly considered a *Christian* celebration of Jesus, and it is slowly but surely being "outlawed" *because* of Jesus? We're supposed to say, "Happy Holidays" instead of "Merry Christmas," so as not to offend anyone! It seems the Christians took the pagan holiday, gave the day the Lord had made back to Him to honor Jesus, and now that it is, Satan's not happy and the easiest way for him to be rid of it is to take it back again, claiming the day is really pagan after all, so you Christians really don't want it. It's not what God has for you. Just some thoughts...

Charles Spurgeon, who I greatly admire, also spoke out against Christmas. He said it is vain and worldly. Let's look at contrasts here. Probably in his day, the world was more focused on the things of God than this world today is. We are leaning way far into the favor of Satan than we are God, in many instances. So, I hate to admit this, but for us today, Christmas and Easter may be as godly as we can get as a country. For some, it is their only two days in church all year. If we cancel Easter and Christmas as Christian celebrations, some would just cancel church altogether. Is that what our Father in Heaven desires? If someone were only going to come and see you twice a year, would you say, "No, thanks; I don't want to see you at all then." Maybe with just those two days

Oh, Holy Night

a year, it could work into a closer relationship with the Savior, having been given the opportunity.

I also read this quote, "Why is it necessary to drag His holy name in connection with what takes place at the season of carnal jollification?" Okay, let's think about that. Where did Jesus go when He walked this earth? He went right into Matthew's house for dinner - a known sinner/tax collector. He spoke to the woman at the well, a known adulteress, living with someone who was not her husband. He was where He "shouldn't" have been, most times. Why? Because greater is He wherever He goes, than is he (Satan) in this world! Satan has no power when **Jesus enters in.** Praise God and Hallelujah!! And joy comes from our Lord, and no where else!

But the shopkeepers, they make so much money this time of year. Isn't it about greed? Well, we all have high seasons in our businesses. Even the tax accountants are super busy leading up to April 15th each year. And most times when we are out shopping, we are buying for ourselves. Isn't it refreshing to have other people's names on our list, and to think about what would bring them joy? Taking the focus off ourselves, and putting it on another's needs is usually a good thing. Love God and love others! It may be a stretch here...but I'm fighting to take Christmas back for we Christians. Can you tell?

Some want to compare our worship of Jesus on Christmas, to those that worshipped the golden calf at Mt. Sinai, when Moses took a little too long coming back down from the mountain. Okay, focus...where is our focus? They were bowing down, and dancing around, and feasting about a golden calf. Do we think they had the slightest inkling that they were in the wrong? They would have to have been totally stupid not to truly realize it. But it's a choice they decided to make. Are we so in the wrong to put our focus on Jesus, and feast around His birth, and give presents to each other in honor of His gift to us in this world? We Christians aren't worshiping Santa Claus...at least I hope not! Even for those that don't know Jesus, maybe this is as close to thinking about the Savior of the world as they will get in the year? Who knows? But if we give Christmas back to the pagans, then what do we do on December 25th…sit and twiddle our thumbs making a point that THIS IS NOT ABOUT JESUS! What message does that really convey to the non-believers? We should be saying, OUR LIVES ARE TOTALLY ABOUT JESUS EVERY DAY! And we have the freedom to celebrate Him any day of the year. Do we want to "appear" to be in bondage, while they "appear" to be free?--when exactly the opposite is true! We have been set free in Christ! That's to be celebrated! The world didn't recognize Him when He came. "Even in his own land and among his own people, he was not accepted. John 1:11 (NLT) John pointed him out to the people. He shouted to the crowds, "This is the one I was talking about…" John 1:15 (NLT) We, like John, want to be there on Christmas day to say, "This Jesus is the one we are talking about!"

There are certain things we should and shouldn't do. We all know that. But if our greatest crime is that we celebrate Jesus' birth on an originally pagan holiday, taking that day away from Satan and putting it back as the Lord's day in our hearts and minds, is that so terribly wrong as Christians? My husband Jim said, "I don't mind if someone gets Phil's birthday wrong, or even spells his name with two "l's. What really matters is that they are remembering our son who died." I have to agree. If you get some of the facts wrong in remembering him, it is okay, but at least attempt to honor that he lived! One friend recently said, "I am so very thankful to have this season with my family. It is one of the few times I can lift up the name of Jesus and feel that they may be listening. I can actually read from my Bible the story of the Lord's birth. It is amazing. It is a precious opportunity."

It may be a proven fact that Christmas "time" is tied into the winter solstice, sun worshipers and Saturn, meaning Satan. Didn't God make winter, the sun and Saturn too…and even Satan himself? What Satan takes away to mean for harm, God can take back and use for good, every single day. I feel like we are bowing down to Satan, and giving him what he wants. I don't want to do that. "For the law was given through Moses; God's unfailing love and faithfulness came through Jesus Christ." John 1:17 (NLT)

Oh, Holy Night

As you can see, this SAND Room message is longer than normal. There was a lot to cover, and I tried to keep it short. Some will agree with what I have to say here, and some will not. But it makes me think about Mary after the birth of Jesus, and how she, "quietly treasured these things in her heart and thought about them often." Luke 2:19 (NLT) I think about this often, and I treasure the gift of Jesus every day in my heart. I wanted to share these thoughts with you, so you can think about them too. Maybe, just maybe, our Father in Heaven is asking us to celebrate His Son each day, including December 25th, because He is so deserving of all of our attention, our worship, and our praise always!

Have an Oh, Holy Night, and a Holy every day, too. And when **S**earching **A**nd **N**oticing the **D**ivine this year, let's let it be Jesus that the world notices about us, at all times, and in all ways, as we honor His Holy Birth *every single day*. Amen

31

Surprise!

I woke up Christmas morning to quite a surprise…but I don't think it's what you might expect. I woke up to find my husband *missing* from our home. Yes, GONE! It was 6:30 a.m., still dark outside, and I was wandering around our place looking for him. He had "disappeared"! And you'll never guess, unless you know me well, what was running through my mind… I had thoughts of the rapture. "Had Jim been taken Home to Heaven by our Savior on Christmas Day?" And if so, "Why was I still here?" I got to experience, for just a moment, what it might be like to not be "ready" when Jesus comes for those that believe in Him as their Savior.

Now, these thoughts were quick, and not to such an extent of panic that I ran screaming from my house waking the neighbors. But suffice it to say, it made for an interesting few moments…until I looked to see if Jim's phone was still beside his bed, and it wasn't. So I called him, and he answered to tell me that he was on his way home. You see, Jim maintains ATM's, and he was working on Christmas Day. Since he already had some calls come in, in the wee morning hours, he decided to go out and fix them so he could be with us all at the kids' house at 7:30, enjoying the festivities of the day.

So, no rapture…just broken ATM's. But this is an experience I wanted to share with all of you, especially after reading the book, "Four Blood Moons," by John Hagee. I am not in complete agreement with all that Hagee had to say, but most of it. I can't possibly go into all that the book contains here. But after reading it, I believe 2014-2015 could be quite a time in earth's history for Israel, and also all who call on Jesus as Lord, especially when we

Surprise!

consider, *The sun will be turned to darkness and the moon to **blood** before the coming of the great and dreadful day of the Lord.* (Joel 2:31 NIV) Hagee asks at the end of his book, "Are you ready?" Are we? Are we ready to meet Jesus, whatever day He may come back for His church? I want to be, because, *Two men will be working together in the field; one will be taken, the other left.* (Matthew 24:40 NLT) I don't want to be left here *toiling* on earth when the best party of all time is going on in Heaven!!

When **S**earching **A**nd **N**oticing the **D**ivine, you have to ...*look up and lift up your heads, because your redemption draws near.* (Luke 21:28) *For you know quite well that the day of the Lord's return will come unexpectedly, like a thief in the night .* (1 Thess. 5:2 NLT) Jim was GONE, like a thief had come in the middle of the night and taken him. I hadn't heard a thing… I had to ask myself in those few moments of not finding him, "Was I not ready?" Have you ever asked yourself the same question? "Am I ready and waiting for Jesus' return?" *He will come again, not to deal with our sins, but to bring salvation to all who are eagerly waiting for him.* (Hebrews 9:28b NLT) Amen!

32

The Open Door

She reached out to turn the door knob, heading back into the house, when she heard God's gentle whisper, "This is the open door." It was unmistakable, and yet she wanted to refuse God's prompting. The very prompting she had been waiting for…the very opportunity she had asked God to give her. She wanted to ignore it. But she couldn't. It was time. It was time to speak to her ex-husband about some things that had been on her heart for so long. They were finally there, together, and alone, which rarely ever happened. God was clearly giving her the perfect opportunity to apologize for some things that had taken place so many years ago - things that were less than the godly woman she desires to be. With so much water under the bridge, she knew she needed to now cross over that bridge and offer up some humble pie…to clear the air of painful things that could keep a heart tethered to unworthiness when it's time for the bread and the cup of remembrance.

> *So anyone who eats this bread or drinks this cup of the Lord unworthily is guilty of sinning against the body and blood of the Lord. That is why you should examine yourself before eating the bread and drinking the cup.*
> 1 Corinthians 11:27-28 (NIV)

It seems when God calls us to a time of humility, it is for ourselves. He wants to free us from what is tying us to the past. God has so much waiting for us…things we would miss out on if not for humbling ourselves before Him and obeying even when everything in our flesh cries out, "NO! Not now! I don't want to!" As hard as it may be to obey, it is harder still not to. Those times of disobedience are the things that will eat away at us like a cancer. God so longs for us to live free of Satan's grasp on our heart, and

The Open Door

on our soul…if we would only listen and obey. In this situation, her ex-husband had some things to bring to the table of forgiveness also. When she opened up to him, he was not so much interested in *her* past transgressions towards him, as he was in *his* towards her. To say she was surprised might be an understatement! Both were blessed on this day in unexpected ways. He, in knowing she cared enough to admit her failings, and she, in hearing that he would have done many things differently, also. Life had moved on…new marriages, children grown, and the grandchildren they share. But with a new forgiveness in their relationship, there is more enjoyment in the life they now have. The hands of time couldn't be turned back. What had happened couldn't be undone. But in Christ, they could freely move forward into all that God has planned for those who love Him and are called according to His purpose! (Romans 8:28)

In **S**earching **A**nd **N**oticing the **D**ivine today, let's all take some time to search our hearts and watch for God's open doors, wherever and whatever they may be. When we are called to obedience, it's usually not easy, but it's always well worth it! There are an untold number of blessings waiting on the other side of our obedience to our Father in Heaven.

33

We Prayed A Lot

What do you do when you are on vacation with your best friend? Do you do a lot of shopping, site seeing, drinking coffee, drinking alcohol, exercising, talking, all of the above, none of the above? I recently returned home from Florida, having spent ten days with my best friend. Thinking back over our time together, what came to me was that we prayed a lot! That makes me chuckle to write that because you might think we had a horrible time together and it took a lot of prayer to get through it! Quite the opposite is true. We always have a great time together doing many different things. But our times together have changed over the last 20 years or so. We used to ski, play racquetball, bowl, and play softball a lot. Yes, we were quite active. We lived in Germany when we met. Life was good, full of fun and lots of activities. I was much more of a sports nut then than a God nut…if you want to put it that way. Thankfully, as the years have gone by, we have both grown in our faith, and now our God times together are usually our best times together…especially if they can be on a beach, with a cup of coffee, watching the east coast sun rise…if I have gotten up early enough to join her!

Some may say, how boring—reading the Bible and praying with your best friend. What a way to spend a vacation! Maybe you can think of a thousand things more exciting than that. There was a time when I would have been one of those people. Now, I'm not saying that all the other activities that we used to enjoy together aren't still awesome. Although, being 20-plus years older, we aren't quite so agile. But what I'm sharing with you here is that praying together, and being in the Word together, is very enjoyable also!

We used to exercise more physically, using our competitive racquetball muscles for fun! Now we exercise more spiritually, wanting God to grow our heart muscle for Him!

Deb and I have experienced a lot of life together over the last 20–plus years…the good, the bad, and the ugly. She has seen me through my darkest days of saying good-bye to our youngest son. We have laughed together, cried together, and we have embraced Jesus together in the midst of it all. One of Deb's friends was diagnosed with Leukemia while I was with her on this last visit. Deb's friend has become my friend too. Jackie knew me through our son's battle with Leukemia. God allowed us to share that day, and that tough diagnosis together…and pray. What would we do, if we couldn't pray? We need one another, to encourage each other, and to pray for each other in Jesus' name. As we do, Jesus will continue to be the glue that holds all of us together!

When **S**earching **A**nd **N**oticing the **D**ivine today, this is where my *search* led. I like what I have *noticed*. I like that friends can share *divine* moments together, and that God grows friendships in this way. Because, *Though one may be overpowered, two can defend themselves. A cord of three strands is not quickly broken.* (Eccl 4:12) I like that…**a lot**!

34

Undeserved

I wake this morning in a bed I don't own. I look out at a spectacular view that I didn't create. I enjoy a coffee maker that I didn't buy. I sit by a fire that I didn't build. And I thank a God that I haven't seen, but One who has given me all these gifts and so many more. My heart is full to overflowing, and I know as I read His Word that this is all small potatoes compared to everything He has waiting for those who love Him.

I did nothing to deserve what I am enjoying today, except for one thing…I got to know someone. I made a friend years ago, and she has brought me here to Tahoe. It's only because of who I know, not because of what I know. It's only because of time spent with someone else, not because I worked so hard to earn these things. I watch the sunrise over the mountains glistening on the lake, and I am thankful as I look out on what God designed. And I realize that nothing here even compares to what is to come for those who believe in the eternal life our Father in Heaven has offered us through His Son, Jesus Christ.

How do we gain the things of Heaven? How do we live in the beauty our Father has waiting for us? How do we attain all the things our heart's desire, but are so far out of reach? We *believe*. We can't work for the things of Heaven. We just have to believe they are there waiting for us. We can't earn our eternal rewards. We just have to open up our hearts and receive them. We can't build our Heavenly Home…it's beyond the reach of our hands here on earth, and what our minds can fathom. We just have to enter into a friendship with our Savior, and watch what happens!

Undeserved

When I think back on the simple beginnings of many of my friendships, I could not have known where those relationships would take me…emotionally, spiritually, and literally physically to many different locations. I met my friend, Aimee, the one who brought me to this lakeside home, at a women's retreat where we were put in a small group together. Then later we simply got up to go to the restroom at the same time, and stood in line next to each other. It started out with a simple conversation, and it has brought me here today to bask in things I do not deserve, but am able to enjoy because we are friends. *"Abraham believed God, and it was credited to him as righteousness," and he was called God's friend."*
James 2:23 (NIV)

In **S**earching **A**nd **N**oticing the **D**ivine this morning, I gazed out the window at the morning's sunrise while lying in a big soft bed. I like to joke with my husband in times like these that, "This is the life to which I am accustomed." But in reality, when I sent my Mom a picture of the view out my window a few days ago, she said, "Not bad for a poor little country girl." I know I am in a place that *someone else* worked hard for. Because of that, it reminds me that Jesus worked hard for us, too, dying on the Cross so that we could have an eternal home in Heaven. Our friendship with Jesus holds so much more than any earthly blessings ever will. Our Lord has gone to prepare a place for us beyond our wildest dreams…if we will simply **call Him Friend**! Heaven will be undeserved. But it doesn't matter; it's still ours when we *believe*. If *you* don't know Jesus as your Friend just yet, it can begin with a simple conversation, and grow into something beyond your imagination. Just say, "Good morning, Jesus. I want to get to know You. Can we start today?"

35

What Do You See?

"What do you see?" It's a great question when riding along on a catamaran off the coast of Cancun. Normally, the response would be, "Beautiful aqua-blue water and puffy-white clouds…maybe even a dolphin or two." But that was not the correct answer on this day as my friend, Denise, sat with a woman she didn't know. When the raindrops started falling, the rest of the guests had gone for cover leaving the two of them alone on deck. This was a divine appointment—most unexpected. But Denise was taking notice of what Jesus had in mind.

When on vacation, it can be relaxing. Jim and I just got back from North Carolina, and there was little pressure, and a lot of quiet couple time. It was fun to not have a schedule, and see things we had never seen before. We had much the same time when we visited Cancun over ten years ago. We did not go to party, as Cancun can be known for. We were not in the party mood. Our son had recently gone Home to Heaven, and we just longed for quiet time on the beach, in the sun, soaking up the Son. That is what we found. That is not what my friend found. She saw much too much of the party scene, and it was not what she wanted, nor needed. As the days went on, her heart was searching for a filling of God. This is not to say she was not enjoying herself; she surely was. But it reminds me of our pastor talking about visiting the Holy Land recently. After many days of being on the "go," he was ready to just hole up in his hotel room and be in the Word. Yes, even in the Holy Land, we need to get alone with God.

God knows our every need. And He will take care of us in the most unusual of ways, as Denise found out on the catamaran that day. She had offered to take a picture of a young couple, and when he

What Do You See?

went off to get a drink, she asked the woman if he was her husband or boyfriend? The woman responded with, "I don't know what he is." It seems they had broken up after booking the trip, and decided to make the trip anyway. She said he had made her cry every day so far. My friend said, "I could tell he might be a challenge." That's when the woman scooted right up next to her and replied with, "Really? What do you see?" Denise had the eyes and heart of Jesus. She saw a need. And when the rain began to fall, and the rest of the crowd headed for cover, she was able to listen to this young woman's struggles and encourage her. Even though Denise had her own needs, she still took the time to sit with this woman and be "Jesus" to her. By encouraging another, she, herself, was filled beyond measure. This woman's problems were not solved on one catamaran ride. No one's will be. But it will be a moment in time that will be long remembered as a blessing to both women.

When **S**earching **A**nd **N**oticing the **D**ivine on vacation, sometimes we will see that the highlight may not be a snorkeling trip, or a party scene...it may be in connecting with a stranger—because just as Jesus calmed the storm when in the boat with His disciples, He can be the calming force in hearts still today.

He got up and rebuked the wind and the raging waters;
the storm subsided, and all was calm.
Luke 8:24 (NIV)

36

My Bad!

My bad...not an expression I normally use, but one I have heard from the younger generation. It is fitting today as I share this story with you, after what I did this morning. What happened was truly "my bad." I was out of line. It wasn't a terrible thing...but it showed what can happen when we turn and go in the opposite direction of what's right. This was the scenario...

Jim and I were headed to church. I was driving, and we needed gas. We pulled into a gas station and the pumps that filled on the left, which is what our car needs, were all full. I chose to swing the car around and come at the pumps in the opposite direction—totally disregarding the arrows that pointed in the other direction. My thinking..."It's Sunday morning, it's quiet, and we will be quick...it won't make any difference." Immediately, a car pulled in behind us, in the wrong direction. I thought, "Uh oh, now I've encouraged another car to go against the arrows. And then, as I sat in the car while Jim pumped the gas, I saw another car pull in. The driver of that car looked at what was going on, and she proceeded to swing her car around in the wrong direction, too! Seriously? I had opened a floodgate of going against the arrows. Is this a small thing on the grand scale of life? Yes! But, it is a good example of what can happen in our lives when we aren't in line with God's will.

God's Word says, *Don't you realize that this sin is like a little yeast that spreads through the whole batch of dough?* (1 Corinthians 5:6 NLT) When something gets off, when someone heads off in the wrong direction, or pulls in against the arrows, as I had done, it can suddenly seem "right" for everyone else. That little bit of "rebellious spirit" spreads so quickly! That is why it is so important to hold each other accountable in our walk with God. We are like sheep. We follow each other most times, instead of following God directly. We shouldn't be looking around to see what everyone else is doing, and judging our actions by theirs. That's dangerous! It's so important to know what God's Word says about EVERYTHING, so that when the world, or even one individual says, "I'm wandering off this way," we will know if that's a wise and godly choice to make. If what's going on doesn't line up with God's "arrows," pointing us in the right direction, we need to stop immediately and line up with God's Word!

When **S**earching **A**nd **N**oticing the **D**ivine, it's easy to miss the Divine if we're watching others and not paying attention to the Word. A whole herd of sheep can wander off a cliff, following one after the other, if their eyes are on the other sheep, and not on the Shepherd. Our "bad" can be contagious, just as mine was this morning! I got the message, Lord. Next time, I'm following the arrows!

37

Pray and Wait

As a writer, I love it when I'm having a conversation with someone and God gently whispers to me, *"Listen."* I know something good is coming, and He wants me to pay close attention! That's what just happened again tonight as I talked with my best friend on the phone. She is visiting her mom and sister, and we were talking about all the things friends talk about. I asked her how her trip went with her sister, and how the concert was? She said, "Did I tell you it was free?" I said, "No, you didn't! How did that happen?" And that's when God whispered, *"Listen,"* as she began to tell me this story…

Deb and her sister, Shirley, headed to Tulsa for a night away. They had high hopes of seeing Dwight Yoakum in concert, but things were not looking good. Not only was the Hard Rock Café Hotel completely booked for the night, so was Dwight's concert there. Someone had told Shirley to call back and ask about any extra tickets, but when Deb did, she actually got a very rude person on the phone telling her that there are **no** extra tickets…they don't do things like that. Once a ticket is sold, it is out of their hands! That didn't stop Deb from praying about it though. She simply asked God if He could please get them tickets.

Deb and Shirley booked a room across the street, and then headed to the Hard Rock. They arrived at the Will Call window and asked if there were any tickets left? There were not. But the lady did tell them to go to the Box Office and wait. She said she might have something left when everyone had gone in. Deb stood by the Box Office, and Shirley stood off at a distance, watching everyone enter into the concert. Others were asking at the Box Office for tickets, but none were to be had. So no one else waited around. Deb said she just stood there, quietly and patiently. They could hear the concert starting inside, and people were still streaming in. Two men came up to the Box Office and said that two tickets had been put aside for them by Dwight...they looked around, found two tickets in separate places and gave them to the men. Let's just say their attitude was not one of gratitude, but more of rudeness...and in they went. Deb could hear a commotion about 15 people who had double-booked seats. After that was settled, it seemed all available tickets were finally gone. But God had other plans for Deb and Shirley. The person at the Box Office then simply handed over two tickets, seats together, and told them there was no charge, and with no explanation. Deb offered to pay, but was told once again, "They are free." So the two sisters went in, thanking God all the way!

When **S**earching **A**nd **N**oticing the **D**ivine, sometimes it's as simple as *listening* when someone else is speaking. Deb said, "All I did was **pray and wait**." We can then *hear* the Divine at work when some, like David, exclaim, *"I waited patiently for the Lord to help me, and he turned to me and heard my cry."* (Psalm 40:1) Let's pray, and not walk away from the "Box Office" before God has a chance to answer our prayers.

38

Where's Your Bible?

"Where's your Bible?" That question was asked of me recently by my six year old granddaughter, Laila. We were just getting in the car to drive over to my other granddaughter, Denell's, soccer game. Laila went looking for one of my Bibles that I keep in the car, and it was not in its usual place. She asked me, "Where's your Bible, Oma?" I said to her, "It's up here, and then I handed it to her in the backseat." That started our discussions about God…

This drive to the soccer game was about seven minutes long. But in that short period of time, much happened! Laila asked me how she could know God was here if she couldn't see Him? I asked her if she knew the feeling of being loved? She said she did. I said to her, "Then you can feel God, because God is Love." I told her that even though we can't see God, He is all around us and lives in us, too, like the air and the wind. Laila was very serene on this day, seemingly very interested in the things of God. I wondered if it was time…I asked Laila if she would like to ask Jesus to come and live in her heart? She said that she would. And right there in the car while driving along, we prayed through knowing that Jesus is the Son of God…that He died on the Cross to take the punishment for the things we do wrong in our lives so we don't have to be punished. We continued to pray about Jesus rising from the dead, and that when we believe in Him and ask Him to come and live in our hearts, we will live forever in Heaven with Him. She repeated everything sweetly and calmly after me. I then asked her to take a deep breath…she did. I said, "Do you see how full you feel? That is God living inside of you." But this was not the end of the conversation, or the day…

Laila continued to ask questions about Heaven on our short drive. I told her that everyone dies, but when Jesus lives in our hearts we don't really die, we move to Heaven where her Grandpa and Uncle

Phil are. I told her that I will probably go to Heaven before her…to which she replied, "Oh NO!" But I told her that is just the way it usually is, and that I would not want her to be sad for a long time because I will be happy living in Heaven. When we got back to her house after the game, Laila wanted me to color with her. I drew an apple tree, and she did too. She wanted to put the date on her drawing, so she did. Then she drew me another picture…it was of a rainbow. She handed it to me, and she said, "I want you to give this to Jesus when you see Him." I took both pictures home with me that day, along with another one she had done of the tracing of her hand. I have them here now, in my Bible. One day, when I have moved on to Heaven, she will have these drawings as a sweet memory of our time together!

When **S**earching **A**nd **N**oticing the **D**ivine, it doesn't have to take very long…perhaps just a seven-minute drive. When asked, "Where is your Bible?", let's make sure it is handy! From there, many lessons can be learned, and even passed on to future generations.

For the Lord is good and his love endures forever;
his faithfulness continues through all generations.
Psalm 100:5 (NIV)

39

Gifts of Love

Many have heard of the "Five Love Languages." It's interesting to find out what they are, and how they match up with not only ourselves, but those around us. I was having this very conversation with a gal at work the other day. She said her husband had given her flowers for Valentine's Day. And then she said, "Just roses." I quickly replied, "Just ROSES? That is awesome!" She then told me he had also cleaned the kitchen for her, and that he could skip the flowers if he would just clean the kitchen for her every day. I asked her if she had heard about love languages. She had not. But after I told her, she said she was going to get the book and read it. She is newly married, so that might be good!

Speaking of Valentine's Day, I had my grandchildren here this year, and we were supposed to have a "gala event" in celebrating the day. The only problem is, I didn't know what we were going to do during this "gala event." They were excited, and I was bewildered. I'm not big on shopping, decorating, cooking, etc… I prefer something more simple, probably more in line with my love language which is *quality time*. But the kids wanted more than that, and God knew that. And God knows me! So what did He do? He had one of my good friends bring me everything I needed for this gala event, and she wasn't even aware of it. Rene' walked into work with a bag full of Valentine's Day goodies. There were marshmallow hearts to make, (I had never made marshmallows.) heart-shaped pasta with red sauce, sparkling apple cider, Lego's, and one other gift I will tell you about in a bit. This friend's love language is *gifts,* and she had given me gifts of love to share with those I love. It was amazing!

This became a Valentine's Day to remember with the grandchildren because of God's provision through a friend. When we are at a loss, God is never at a loss, He knows what is needed! I love to see how much our God loves us in the way He cares for the details of our lives. *Let them give thanks to the Lord for his unfailing love and his wonderful deeds for mankind...* (Psalm 107:8)

I didn't have to go far when Searching And Noticing the Divine on this Valentine's Day. It came in a large red bag full of gifts of love. To not notice how God uses others to bless our lives, we would be sadly remiss. We all have different gifts in the Body of Christ, just as we all have different love languages. No one person has them all. But when we are connected to the Body of Believers, we can see how God orchestrates each person's spiritual gift to help and encourage one another. And what was the last gift I haven't told you about? It was a small felt heart with a recording device in it. I saved it until it was time for the Oregon grandkids to make their trek home after a week-long visit. I recorded a message to be played when they got in the car. They were sad to be leaving, but this made the departure easier. I have a Valentine's Day heart of gratitude for all the things I wouldn't have thought of, but God did! Thank You God, and thank you Rene'!

40

One Pair of Shoes

Have you ever gone looking for just one pair of shoes? Of course, we all have. But have you ever gone looking in a place where you didn't think there were any shoes, hoping to find some? That's what we did recently, and we were once again astounded at how the Lord goes before us on our path!

When I found this verse in Proverbs 4:25, "Look straight ahead, and fix your eyes on what lies before you," it took me back to that moment in time…and to that one pair of shoes we needed! My daughter-in-law, Cami, and I had headed over to a CVS Pharmacy in search of a pair of shoes for Cooper, age three. We had arrived in Monterey with the whole family, all set to visit the aquarium, when it was discovered that Cooper's shoes had been left at home. After some very rainy days, they were wet, and the plan was to dry them out in the car on the way there. But, they had been forgotten—and it wasn't discovered until we had paid to park the car, and were getting out that there were no shoes for Cooper. We had remembered that we had seen a CVS Pharmacy within walking distance of the parking lot, so off we went, looking for just one pair of shoes to get Cooper through the day. As we approached the only place in the store that had shoes of any kind, we saw a very small, black pair of shoes sitting on the bottom of the rack. I remember my eyes fixing on them! Above the shoes were some hooks that held flip-flops and some water shoes, all too big for our little Cooper. Could it be that God had placed this one pair of very needed black shoes there in the perfect size for Cooper? He had! They fit! So without much delay, we were able to make our way back over to the aquarium to rejoin the rest of the family for a day of fun.

One Pair of Shoes

What do we do with this simple moment in time, and this seemingly small provision? Do we skip over it and go on with our day? Or do we stop for just a moment, and thank God for once again watching over us in such detail? If we don't remember to thank God for the seemingly small things in life, will we remember to thank Him when the bigger things come along? Where do we rule God out of the details, and where do we include Him in? Or is God in all things, at all times? Isaiah 65:24 says, *"I will answer them before they even call to me. While they are still talking about their needs, I will go ahead and answer their prayers!"* On the quick walk over to CVS, Cami and I were still talking about our needs...and God had gone ahead to answer them! That's fun to see! Sometimes, we see prayers answered with a, "Yes," and sometimes a, "No," or even a, "Wait." But...

If we are truly **S**earching **A**nd **N**oticing the **D**ivine each day, I believe we will see God's provisions more and more no matter what His answer is! *In all things God works together with those who love him to bring about what is good. (Romans 8:28)* On this day, one small pair of shoes was very good!!

41

Whose Scent Are We Wearing?

God took me into Ephesians the other morning, and I wondered why? What would I find there that I hadn't seen before? Recently my friend, Lynn, who is memorizing the book of James reminded me how rich, and full, and alive the Word of God is! After all the times she has been through James in her memorization process, God is still showing her new things. We will never reach the depths of all that God has for us to learn in His Word! So into Ephesians I went, to chapter five, verse two, where it talks about Jesus giving himself as a sacrifice to take away our sins, and that sacrifice was like *sweet perfume* to His Father in Heaven. (NLT) And then I knew why I was in Ephesians. I hadn't been smelling like sweet perfume. The "world" had dumped some of its garbage on me, and I had been choosing to wear it for a while. Then I realized I could also *choose* to dump it out with the rest of the world's stench! When Christ lives in us, we don't have to wear anything but His love and forgiveness in our lives.

I talked to a friend who knows someone going through a very difficult and ugly divorce. The "stench" from what is happening is weighing heavy on her. She is pulling away from her home church, and from activities that she used to enjoy. Why? I think because her soon-to-be ex-husband's garbage has piled up on her, and she thinks she has to wear it for at least a certain length of time. But it's **not** her garbage! The things he is choosing to do, she doesn't have to wear! When I think of this woman, who I have met a few times, she has always worn the sweet aroma of Christ. I told my friend, "Please tell her not to wear his garbage. It's only the enemy who wants her clothed in that!" In 2 Corinthians 2:15 it says, "For we are to God the pleasing aroma of Christ…"

This reminds me of the Charlie Brown character, Pigpen. Everywhere he goes, a cloud of dirt follows him. As believers in the saving grace of Jesus Christ, that **should not be us**. We should sparkle! As we sang in church this morning, "Sin had left a crimson stain…He washed me white as snow." God's mercies are new every morning!

God's amazing Word is our instruction manual through life. We are told to live in the Truth, so that "…Satan might not outwit us. For we are not unaware of his schemes." (2 Corinthians 2:11) Satan stinks up the world. We are aware of that. But that doesn't give him the power to stink up the Church, which is the Body of Christ! Let's boot Satan's garbage to the curb and say "adiós," which means "to God" in Spanish. God will handle it for us!

When **S**earching **A**nd **N**oticing the **D**ivine, let's take notice of whose scent we are wearing each day. Is it the pleasing aroma of Christ underneath the strong Armor of God, or are we unwittingly wearing the world's garbage that has been thrown in our vicinity? Every day can be garbage day. All we have to do to put the "cans" out is to open our hearts up to the Truth of God's Word, and let it wash us white as snow!

42

Let's Take a Walk!

It is a beautiful day here in Northern California, in the high 60's, and sunny. I have been in the house a lot in the past week, working on some things. Today, it seemed God was encouraging me to take a walk. I put my shoes on, got my sunglasses, and headed out the back door for the Iron Horse Trail. We are blessed to have this magnificent paved trail right by where we live. It stretches far north and south of here, and it is a favorite place for cyclist and walkers/joggers of all ages. On the weekends, it's practically a "traffic jam" out there! Today, it was quiet, being that it is a Monday afternoon.

As I started out, I wondered where I would meet God along the trail. I was discussing some things with Him, and I was glad the trail was pretty empty so no one could hear me talking to "myself" as I walked along. I have heard we can't fight a thought with a thought…we need to speak things out of our mouth, so it goes into our ears, and then enters our head to renew our mind. That is what I was doing! It was fun to be out in the sun, and searching for God's divine presence today. Of course, He was in the cotton-candy clouds, far off green hills, and wild flowers along the path. But I wondered if I'd get a new SAND Room writing on my walk. God didn't disappoint me! I did! Here it is!

When I got about 20 minutes down the trail, I entered into a part of the trail that goes through the city. There were some benches there. I decided to sit a spell. That's when I realized there was a thrift store right next to me. Uh oh!! I should have listened when it passed through my mind to bring some cash before I left the house. My pockets were empty… But I decided to go take a look in the thrift shop anyway.

Let's Take A Walk!

My husband, Jim, had been asking me to find a piece of material for the train layout he's working on. Wouldn't you know it! I found the perfect thing for him! It was only $5.00! What a deal! I went to the counter to ask if they could hold it for me! I figured I could walk the 20 minutes back home, get some cash, and be right back. They told me they don't hold items, *and* they were closing in 15 minutes. They were very nice about it. But still, the answer was, "No." That's when "God" showed up. A lady who was shopping heard my predicament, and offered to loan me the $5! Was I ever happy!! She didn't know me from Adam, but she trusted me just the same. It wasn't a lot, but it meant a lot to me! She was, *"... rich in good works and generous to those in need, always being ready to share with others.* 1 Timothy 6:18 (NLT)

I went out on a **S**earching **A**nd **N**oticing the **D**ivine walk today, and enjoyed *noticing* God's provision - both in finding what Jim needed, and meeting a generous person who was there at the right time to help me out! *Whenever you seek him, you will find him.* (2 Chronicles 15:2) I'm kind of glad I neglected to take money with me today...it allowed me to see God's provisional blessings. That was probably on **His** path all along!

43

Is Your Gas Light On?

How often have we wondered if we are where God would have us be? There are so many paths in life to follow, and so many choices to make on those paths… God gives us the freedom to choose—even considering our eternal life with Him. It is not a forced "issue." We either choose to follow Jesus Christ, or we don't. If we think we haven't made a choice about Jesus yet, the truth is, we have. To *not* choose Him is actually a choice. That choice will count when we stand before our Lord on our last day. Will Jesus be our advocate on that day, pronouncing us forgiven because of His death and resurrection, or will He say, "I never knew you"? That is an important choice that we all need to think about sooner rather than later.

As we make choices, there can be things in life that seem like "coincidences." But my brother, Steve, always calls these "coinciding" events. I like that! As a friend visited our church this last Sunday, unbeknownst to us, there were to be some coinciding events. We entered into church together, and after worship, some announcements were made. The assistant pastor told us a story of years ago when the low gas light in his car came on. He knew his tank was close to empty. When he finally pulled into a gas station, there was little if any gas left in his car. AND, he discovered he didn't have his wallet…no money and no gas. He hated to ask a stranger for money, but he had little choice. He found a very generous "helper" on that day. He asked for $2 for gas, but the man gave him a full tank. What a huge blessing! He went on to encourage us that if we had arrived at church this morning spiritually empty, "gas light on," we were in the right place. We could fill up here. And we sure did! It was a fantastically encouraging, transforming service!

Now, onto the coinciding events of the morning... As the worship music started, they announced a new song we would be doing. I didn't know it. But my friend turned to me and said, "That is the very song I was singing this morning while getting ready for church." Knowing some of the things she is going through right now, I knew it was certainly helping to fill her tank. But what **really** surprised us after the service was when she shared with us that her gas light had come on sometime while driving to church this morning! Coinciding plan of God? I believe so. Any other Sunday, she would have been at her home church. But this morning, God was meeting her at our church. We can take comfort in coinciding events. They help us to know we are right where God would have us be. We can't know all the reasons this side of Heaven as to why, but we can let the Holy Spirit strengthen us with these small personal touches from God!

When **S**earching **A**nd **N**oticing the **D**ivine, let's take notice when things match up in a supernatural way. God is filling our hungry souls and helping us journey on!

What can we say about such wonderful things as these?
If God is for us, who can ever be against us?
Romans 8:31 NLT)

44

Such a Little Thing

How detailed can God get in our lives? I think today He was having fun showing me! I could easily have over looked His help, but I am choosing not to. We are told, "If you are faithful in little things, you will be faithful in large ones. But if you are dishonest in little things, you won't be honest with greater responsibilities." Luke 16:10 (NLT) It seems in God's scope of things, little and big, both are important. I want to be honest, and in line with His will in all things…even if it is seemingly the size of an ant.

Today, as I cleaned up our back yard, sweeping, and trimming, and collecting those trimmings into a bag for disposal, I wasn't looking forward to once again getting pricked by the many thorns on a certain bush. But, like I normally do, I was just going to tough it out, deal with a little blood, and get the job done. I did think, "Maybe one of these years I will actually purchase a pair of gardening gloves," as I continued to work on preparing the yard for this beautiful Spring-like weather we are having.

When it came time to pick up all the clippings, the allergies associated with yard work were kicking in. I came into the house, took an allergy pill, grabbed a plastic grocery bag to use as a "glove" against the thorns, and then headed back out to finish up. As I stepped out the door into the back yard, I looked down and saw some bubble wrap on the ground. I wondered where it had come from. I hadn't seen it before when I was trimming the bushes. A thought passed through my mind, "Maybe I can use that to protect my hand from the thorns?" And when I picked it up, I noticed it wasn't just a piece of bubble wrap, it was in the shape of a bag I could slip my hand into. I laughed to myself and thought, "Maybe this is a new invention for just this sort of thing?" I have to say, it worked pretty well as I scooped up the clippings! There were less thorn pricks than usual! In fact, in thinking about it, I don't know if I actually got pricked at all through the bag. There were some allergic scrapes on my arms, but no blood to be seen!

How do these things happen? How do bubble-wrap bags that can be worn over a hand, just appear in a backyard of thorn-covered clippings? Is God really that much into the details of our lives? Does He really care that much to provide such a thing for His children? I'm going with a big, "Yes, He does!" on this. I have seen God in so many things, in so many ways, and today was no different. No matter how ridiculous, or how small, or how surprising, I don't want to miss a thing He is doing and providing each day!!

Searching **A**nd **N**oticing the **D**ivine might sometimes take on microscopic proportions—But none the less, my heart is grateful no matter how small the gift. My Heavenly Father probably got great joy in the little surprise He left in the yard for me today!

45

A New Perspective

It was long past time to gain some new perspective on a difficult time in my life—to allow God to change my broken way of thinking... Because as God's Word says, "...letting your sinful nature control your mind leads to death. But letting the Spirit control your mind leads to life and peace." Romans 8:6 (NLT) This is a little longer SAND Room message today, but I think it's a very important one! If you'll allow me to share...

Many years ago, as a young mom of three boys, I wasn't the most patient, loving, kind person... I was probably tired, like most young parents are. The thirties can be a busy time of life with children, and ours was no exception. Gentleness was put on the back burner, and, "Just do what I ask you to do" was forefront! "Why? Because I said so, that's why!" How many of us heard that growing up, and vowed to never say it? But we did! Now, fast forward all these years later and our boys are now in their 30's, and with their wives, are each raising their own three children. We are truly blessed - and as a Grandma, the Fruit of the Spirit—love, joy, peace, patience, kindness, etc...are much easier to exhibit. One reason is that I go home at the end of the day to a quiet house, instead of one filled with sports gear, school backpacks, and homework that needs to be finished before baths and bedtime! I think you get the picture. But I still had a problem. The patience I *have* learned, not just because life is quieter, but because I have grown in my faith through the years, is now only shared with two of our grown sons. One son left this world for Heaven 12 years ago. There is no making it up to him with the peace and kindness that God has taught me through the years. There is no loving on his children, or encouraging him in his present life. I missed the "boat" with him so to speak...it sailed, and I was left holding onto the 30-

something-year-old Mom mistakes that I'm not all that proud of. So what did I do with them? I stuffed my mistakes down deep in my soul, covering them up with all of God's goodness and blessings of today, and I figured I would just have to take the mistakes I made with him to the grave with me. Little did I know that God had a better plan with even that mess inside of me—God wanted me to finish that unfinished business. The Holy Spirit, when given complete control of our minds, has a great way of cleaning out the garbage from the past. How? I'll tell you what I have been putting into practice to let the Holy Spirit do His work in me.

I knew that God was capable of healing a shattered heart because I have experienced that, and I am so grateful. But I didn't know how to hand over that dark little box full of "Mom mistakes" that seemed so "right" to hold onto. But in God's Word it says we do **not** have to pay for what has **already** been paid for by Jesus Christ. It is okay, really okay, to ask for forgiveness, and to **receive** that forgiveness. Pride will tell us **we** need to do better to clean up our own mistakes. For me, for this **receiving** process to work, God has been teaching me to include **speaking His Truth out loud, and often**! By speaking truths out loud, they can enter in through our ears, and change our way of thinking! My brain needed to literally break off connections to condemning thoughts by actually speaking things like, "So now there is no condemnation for those who belong to Christ Jesus" Romans 8:1 (NLT), as well as many other truths. This is how mind renewal takes place. Jesus battled Satan by *saying*, "It is Written…" When I do what Jesus modeled, those destructive thoughts start to die, and my mind starts to heal. In practicing this, I am gaining more of the life and peace God's Word promises! I not only thank God out loud for His promises as I drive down the freeway, I thank Him for cell phones, because those in the cars around me don't think I am insanely talking to myself. Little do they know I am on a direct line with God, involved in the best intensive Counseling session ever! I've also warned my husband, Jim, if he hears me whispering in the middle of the night, I'm not talking in my sleep, I'm speaking out truth!

Searching **A**nd **N**oticing the **D**ivine is sometimes as *easy* as seeing God's blessings in an ordinary day. But sometimes, it's as *hard* as abandoning our mistakes at the foot of the Cross and noticing Divine intervention take them away. The enemy's lies make it hard to truly believe what we have been offered through the blood of Jesus. But when we use the Sword of the Spirit, which is the **Spoken** Word (Rhema) of God, there will be amazing results!
"...be transformed by the renewing of your mind."
Romans 12:2 (NLT)
(If you want to know where to start, try speaking out Psalm 103. It has many mind-renewing elements!)

A New Perspective

46

The Very Reason

Why do I send these writings out? Why take the time to notice all the little, and big things God is doing? Why put them down on paper, and share them with others? Okay, I enjoy it; that's one reason. Writing is truly a pleasure for me. But as I talked with my husband, Jim, the other day, I was telling him that The SAND Room's purpose is so that we can *all* see God. It seems when we want God to "show up," it's usually in a time of crisis, and we pray, and we pray hard, perhaps for the first time, maybe for the hundred-thousandth time, "Please God, help us now!" And we wait for Him to do His "thing." And if He doesn't do what we have asked, then we wonder if He is really there after all? But if we can start to get in the practice of seeing God *every* day, in *every* thing, then I truly believe we can start to see Him in the big things we need, even when He "supposedly" doesn't show up—because God is *always* with us. He never leaves us. He never forsakes us…He loves us! Just because we don't always get what we want, or what we ask for, it doesn't mean He has abandoned us. Do we always give our children exactly what they ask for? Or do we give them what would be best for them? God is our Father who knows best, and His plans and purposes far exceed what we can presently understand.

I write about simple things, like bubble wrap showing up in my back yard to save my hands from thorn pricks. I write about miracle healings in ocean waters when a foot has been injured to the bone from the rocks. I write about everything in between. I write about it all, just so that I can not only take note of God myself in all things, but so that you can too. And then I get a response like this from one of my readers, and it truly encourages me to keep writing about all these things.

This one is important for me to see. A lot of times I only think God can operate in our lives in the case of big life altering things. I sometimes leave Him out of things save for the really big stuff. It is good to be reminded that He has a hand in everything and wants to be honored in all things, big and small. To Him goes the glory.

If The SAND Room writings ended today, they could die a happy death by me. Why? Because my purpose has been for readers to notice God's Truth throughout each and every day. And the reader above, who was touched by what was written, was our 35 year old son. Nothing warms a mother's heart more! Psalm 145:4-7 says, "Let each generation tell its children of your mighty acts. I will meditate on your majestic, glorious splendor and your wonderful miracles. Your awe-inspiring deeds will be on every tongue…Everyone will share the story of your wonderful goodness…"

When **S**earching **A**nd **N**oticing the **D**ivine, it is important to share Divine moments with those who know us best—even Jesus had an inner circle with John, then James and Peter.

Let the Good News spread from within, so that soon *everyone will share the story* of God's wonderful goodness!

47

The Year Was...

The year was 1946, June to be exact. My dad, Vincent, was just turning eleven, and living in a sweet little house in Oakland, California. He lived there with his dad and his mom. His older sister, Charmaine, had died at the age of 14 a couple of years earlier from pneumonia/kidney failure. The following April, 1947, my dad's dad died of a sudden heart attack at the age of 61. Their home, which was once filled with family, music and laughter, had changed drastically. The only thing that hadn't changed, and in fact, was strengthening, was the deep faith of my grandmother, Charlotte. I recently acquired her Bible, and I'd like to share a portion of the last letter she wrote to her husband, my grandfather, Jack. It was written on March 11, 1947. He was soon to be returning home from a business trip. The letter was safely tucked away in her Bible all these years... She died at the age of 89 in 1988.

...We are very lonesome, too, dear, and will be glad when Friday arrives. Vincent just came home from school and he is practicing. He is a good pal, and does everything I tell him. He has lots of school work and we do them at night. He also is my little bed partner right now...Am looking forward to Friday so you can hold me in your arms...

One month later, Jack was gone, leaving my grandma and my dad really lonesome in this world, except for each other, and our God, who never leaves us nor forsakes us. Not long after my grandfather passed on, my dad and grandma needed to move out of their little home in Sheffield Village, no longer being able to afford the cost of a home.

Why do I share this tale of my family with you today? Because yesterday, my dad and my brother, Keith, took a drive by the little house in Oakland, and were able to actually enter into the house. The owner, who is the granddaughter of the very people who bought the home from my grandma back in the 40's, still lives there. The house has remained in their family for almost 70 years! And when my brother introduced my dad as the previous owner, the woman exclaimed, "You're the *Vincent*?!" What a welcome home! You see, back in 1946, my dad and his parents had written their names in the cement out back. My grandparents' names have long since disappeared from wear, but "Vincent - June 1946" was still visible in the cement! He was *thee* Vincent they had wondered about for so many years.

When Searching And Noticing the Divine, sometimes we have to wait a *very long* time to see God's mysteries revealed. Many times we think God will never come through for us. But He always will, either on this side of Heaven, or the other. I know my grandma knows that now, because on another small note contained in her Bible, she penned these words, "Make no mistake – eternal life is available to every one if we reach out in faith. I have no fear of death. In fact, I look forward to it with joy and anticipation." Charlotte is now, not only in the loving arms of her husband, Jack, but also in the loving arms of her Savior, Jesus Christ. Perhaps when she saw Jesus, she said, "You're the *Christ*!" I'm sure Jesus gave her a hearty, "Welcome Home! You're name has been *written here* in the Book of Life all these years!"

48

Prove To Me That You Love Me

Prove to me that you love me...don't we often ask that of God? And many times we don't want to *listen* for His answer—we think we already know because we are experiencing days when we don't feel very loved. The world can be so hard and cruel. We wonder where God is a lot of the time. How does a God, that we can't see, prove that He loves us? I believe the answer is found in 1 Corinthians 13. Let's take a look…

As I read recently, sometimes our "demon-strations"/tantrums are the exact opposite needed for finding out how much God and others love us. But what if our reactions to these demonstrations were the same as God's when He describes how *love is* in 1 Corinthians 13…if patience and kindness were evident? We might just catch a glimpse of the way our Father loves us no matter what. Or as Paul writes to the Corinthians in 4:12, if we were to "…bless those who curse us, be patient with those who abuse us, and respond gently when evil things are said about us." We might see the true nature and love of God in those instances. If God's love is never haughty, or selfish, or rude…if His love is not demanding of its own way, not irritable or touchy, and we responded to each other in that way, wouldn't God's love be better seen on this earth? And when others aren't so nice, and we barely take notice, not holding a grudge…God's love might be truly felt. Paul writes that love rejoices whenever truth wins out, as should we as believers in Jesus Christ. True love consists of loyalty no matter what the cost, always believing in someone, always expecting the best of them, and always standing our ground defending them. That is certainly a picture of God's love, proven by what Jesus did for all of us! No matter what it cost Jesus, He defended our eternal life through His death on the Cross! Who doesn't want and need this type of devoted love in their life? We all do! And that's what the Father showed us and reminds us of when we ask Him, "Prove to me that you love me." He gave us His only Son, to die for our sins as proof! When Jesus was on the Cross, He said, "Father, forgive them, for they know not what they do." There is no greater love than that!

God knows what's most important to us—to know His love. And **only** God truly knows what each individual needs, because our Father is the very definition of the word LOVE. He speaks everyone's love language perfectly. If we will notice how closely Jesus' walk on this earth matches up with 1 Corinthians 13, we will **see** how much He really does love us. It's when we take a step of faith into God's kind of love, as opposed to this world's kind of love, that we will discover the true love God has waiting for us.

Searching And Noticing the **Divine love** of God is amazing! Little by little on that search, we will experience God's love demonstrated towards us. When we begin living in what we are being offered, we will then be able to offer it to others who are on their own search for true love.

We love because He first loved us.
1 John 4:19 (NIV)

49

What Are Your Needs?

Do we bring our daily needs to God? Big and little? Do some seem ridiculous to even ask for? And yet, God just might be waiting to surprise us with an answer to those very requests!

Just recently my friend, Jackie was in search of some walking sticks. None of us are getting any younger, and sometimes even new struggles with our health can cause us to make certain changes in our normal way of doing things. Jackie is no exception, and she went looking for a new way of hiking…using some nifty sticks! Being budget conscious, like most of us, she asked a woman she knows who manages a thrift store to keep an eye out for some. The woman responded by telling her that she would, but as long as she had been there she had never had any walking poles come in. You probably already know what I'm going to share with you…a few days later she called and told my friend that she would not believe this, but they got some in that day! Jackie was excited! And the thrift store manager was so surprised! Eighty dollar walking sticks, looking almost new, for the now reasonable price of $15.00!

Don't you just love stories like this? Don't we all wish they were a part of our everyday walk with God? They can be, if we will ask, and receive, and open our eyes to see where our answers are coming from! God is doing these kinds of things every single day. But many days, we are so busy running our own lives we miss what God is doing!! Let's take in a deep breath, and realize that the air in our lungs just arrived from our Father in Heaven. "And the Lord God formed a man's body from the dust of the ground and breathed into it the breath of life. And the man became a living person." Genesis 2:7 (NLT) How do we get so **in**dependent that we forget we are **dependent** on our Creator even for the very air we breathe? It's because we, in the form of Adam and Eve, walked out of God's will in the Garden, and then God had them walk out of the Garden into a fallen world…and that is the world we live in to this day. Those that think they have no need of God…we might challenge them to try and live without the air that God is providing for all of us each day! And we might want to remind each other that one day we will live on a New Earth, and we will not miss one thing that God is doing because we will see Him face to face! We will experience God's goodness towards us without all the barriers that keep us from realizing all that God is providing for us every single moment. What an exciting time in our lives Heaven will be! Yes, *lives*, because we will be fully alive, eternally, in God's presence forevermore!

When **S**earching **A**nd **N**oticing the **D**ivine today, let's focus on our eternal hope in Heaven! Let's not take one single breath for granted, because one day we will be in God's eternal Kingdom where walking sticks will no longer even be needed. We will have perfected Heavenly bodies as we walk along with Jesus!

50

The Luggage Rack Man

Have you ever had a time in your life when you knew God had set up a perfect scenario for His will to be done, and yet you missed what He was asking you to do? I sure have, and I'm going to share one with you here today.

I was on an airplane flying to Florida. We had a stopped in Las Vegas on the way, and that's where it got interesting. When we were just about ready to take off, we got word that all the radar on the west coast had gone down. Planes were grounded, and those flying in were diverted to Arizona. We had no idea how long we were going to be there, so I exited the plane to recharge my phone. I noticed a man on the gangway charging his phone, and realized there were plugs there, so I joined him, and we chatted. He shared with me that he was flying to Orlando to be with his father who was having surgery for cancer. When we reentered the plane, I told him that I would be praying for his dad. He thanked me for that. So far, so good, right?

On the rest of the flight I continued to pray for this man's dad, and for the whole family, knowing what a difficult time it was for all of them. I wanted to talk with him again in Orlando, if possible, and "I thought" the luggage rack area would be a good place. As we headed to the tram that would take us to the terminal, I saw him coming towards me. Then he was standing right next to me, and when we entered the tram we were so close to each other that our luggage was bumping each other…that's when God gently whispered that *now* would be a good time to let him know you have been praying for him. Out of a couple hundred people on the plane, God put him right next to me for our little tram journey. But did I listen to God's prompting? No, I didn't. I had my own idea of

The Luggage Rack Man

when would be a good time to let him know I was continuing to pray for his dad. We then got to the terminal, and he moved back so I could exit ahead of him, and then he got off! He headed out at a breakneck speed, pulling his two pieces of carry-on luggage behind him…and I knew then that I had missed my opportunity to talk with him again…he was gone, not going to the luggage area to retrieve anything. What did I have to do then? Repent and ask for God's forgiveness for my disobedience in this matter, and then receive that forgiveness, which is usually the hardest part. Disobedience is not a good feeling…I have felt it before, but I hope with future "assignments" I will continue the process of getting better at this. God gave me another opportunity at the end of my time in Florida to put my obedience to the test again. That time, I wasn't going to miss it! I acted in obedience! I will share that part of the story in the next SAND Room writing.

On this day suffice it to say, that when **S**earching **A**nd **N**oticing the **D**ivine, sometimes we miss what the *Divine* is doing because we are busy doing our own thing. But God loves us so much, He will always offer us His forgiveness, and give us other opportunities to serve Him with a repentant heart! Stay tuned…

51

The Blessings of Obedience

If you read my last writing, "The Luggage Rack Man," you will have a better understanding of where this story originates. If you haven't, let me just say that I had been given an opportunity by God to be in His will, and I had chosen to be out of His will and in my own will. Which reminds me of a book I was just reading that said something to this effect; we can know when we are in the will of God by being completely willing to be in the will of God. Not a direct quote, but close. After writing the last story about disobedience, I wanted to follow up with a more inspirational one!

I was at the end of my visit in Florida, having been there compliments of a wonderful invitation to speak at a ladies tea. All went well, Praise God, and I would soon be heading back to California. I was staying with my friend. She has a neighbor who recently had a leg amputated. I felt God prompting me one night to go and talk with him. The very next morning I again felt prompted to go pay him a visit. That morning we were talking about those who were not able to make it to the tea, and we were reading in Luke 14 about the Great Feast that so many had been invited to, but gave excuses why they couldn't be there. I continued to read further down in Luke where his master told the man to then go out into the streets of the city and invite the crippled and lame, etc... Yes, God, I hear You Loud and Clear! I KNEW I was not going to ignore talking to the neighbor—not after missing an opportunity in the airport on my way to Florida. I shared this with another friend we were having lunch with. She knew what I had to do. I knew what I had to do. I had two days to do it!

We were all coming home from lunch later that day, in two cars, and the first car down the street was the friend I had shared this

The Blessings of Obedience

with. When she passed the house where the crippled man lived, she saw him and his wife were out front. She knew I would have to stop. Along we came, just a minute or so behind her, and my friend and I saw them out front, too—she asked me if I wanted to stop? OF COURSE I DID! We pulled up, and I opened the door as she called out "Hi" to them. At least they knew I was with her, and not just some stranger. I got out and greeted them both, letting them know that God had put them on my heart…that He loved them, and He cared about them. The husband was not all that interested in my visit, but his wife truly was. She was touched that God had sent me to them, and when I left after just a brief visit, she asked me to come back and see her next time I am in Florida. I surely will!

When Searching And Noticing the Divine, we might not always see the final results of our obedience when God is asking us to do something, but most times we will sense the *Divine* peace of being in His will. We will also *Notice* that there is great joy, even when we are called out of our comfort zone in doing it. I don't normally walk up to strangers in that way. But when called to, and seeing it confirmed in God's Word about the master instructing the man to do the same, I knew what I needed to do, and did it! Praise Jesus!

52

Sea Turtles

It was soon to be my young friend, Kendra's, birthday, so I was on the hunt for something she would enjoy. I spotted a glass with a sea turtle on it. I knew she liked turtles, so I bought it and wrapped it up for her special day. Little did I know what God had planned!

I'd like to give you a little history about my relationship with Kendra. She is actually our youngest son, Phil's, friend. They had a very special relationship in their teenage years. Kendra is now 29 and Phil is in Heaven. They spent many happy hours together skiing, swimming, watching movies, etc… all the things teenagers do. Kendra was always a faithful friend to Phil. She was able to fly out to California from Florida six months before God took Phil Home to Heaven. He was fairly healthy at that time, and they enjoyed a day at the Santa Cruz Beach Boardwalk, and other adventures. Don't tell the law, but I actually took the two of them over to a large parking lot, got out of my convertible Mustang, top down, and let Philip behind the wheel. He and Kendra cruised around the parking lot at about ten miles per hour, as happy as larks. Phil was 15 at that time. That was as close as they got to being on a date together, but dating was not really a part of their relationship. They were just very, very good friends through the years, having met in Germany when both of our families lived there.

On my most recent visit to Florida, Kendra was in town with her husband and daughter, Mia. They had driven down from North Carolina. One evening we all took a trip out to the port to see if any of the cruise ships were heading out. My friend, Deb, took her granddaughter, Mia, to the playground. Kendra and I started to walk out on the long pier…Kendra was in search of sea turtles.

Sea Turtles

"How appropriate is this," I thought, since I was waiting to give Kendra her birthday gift. God blessed us with not just one sea turtle spotting, but three or four. It was hard to tell if they were different ones, or just a couple of the same ones coming up for air by the rocks, as the waves crashed against them. What a treat it was, to share this special time with Kendra! She misses her buddy, Phil, who took her cruising in the parking lot that day. But God still allows the two of us cherished times together all these years later.

Kendra's birthday was the next morning after seeing the sea turtles. When she unwrapped her gift she was so surprised! She thought maybe I had gone out late that night and found the glass. Nope! That was all in God's design! I have to believe God wanted our pier stroll to always be a walk to remember, so He blessed it with *His* perfect gifts!

Searching **A**nd **N**oticing the **D**ivine can be so much fun when we see God going ahead of us as we shop, walking beside us as we search, and being there with us when He surprises us with His goodness each day!

Yes, the Lord pours down his blessings.
Psalm 85:12 (NLT)

ABOUT THE AUTHOR
diane.dcshorepublishing.com

Diane C. Shore lives in Danville, CA with her husband Jim of 38 years. They are enjoying these years together after raising three sons, and now being the grandparents of six. Writing and sharing true stories about God is Diane's passion as God continues to lead her and show her new ways of how He expresses His love toward us each day. Whether it is sitting one-on-one with someone, or speaking to a group, Diane is excited to boldly proclaim the Good News of Jesus Christ and how He works in our daily lives.

Made in the USA
Coppell, TX
02 October 2022